LUCCA

TRAVEL GUIDE 2023-2024

Discover the Timeless Charm of Lucca: Unveiling
History, Culture, and Must-Know Travel Tips Before
Visiting

BY

Brenda R. Nelson

There is a Travel planner as a bonus at the end of this amazing guide.

CONTENT

MY LUCCA VACATION EXPERIENCE

I had always wanted to visit Italy, and when the opportunity arose, I knew I wanted to spend some time in Lucca. I had heard that it was a lovely city with a fascinating history, and I was not disappointed. On a bright August day, I arrived in Lucca. The city was alive with bustle, and I was impressed by the strong feeling of history and culture that pervaded the air. My first day was spent roaming around the Old Town's tiny alleyways, admiring the ancient architecture and enjoying the local food.

I went for a walk around the city walls in the evening. The views from the summit were incredible, and I could see for kilometers in all directions. I felt as if I were in a fairy tale, and I knew I'd never forget this moment. The next day, I went to the Duomo di San Martino, the city's cathedral. The cathedral, which was erected in the 12th century, is one of Italy's most outstanding specimens of Romanesque architecture.

I wandered throughout the cathedral for hours, admiring the stained glass windows and beautiful woodwork. In the afternoon, I attended a cookery lesson at a nearby school. Traditional Tuscan foods such as pasta alla Norma and tiramisu were taught to me. It was a lot of fun learning about the city's food, and I even got to taste some of my creations!

On my last day in Lucca, I went to the Guinigi Tower. The tower is one of the city's most recognizable features and provides breathtaking views of the surrounding countryside. I went to the top of the tower and was rewarded with a breathtaking panoramic view. I was in Lucca for four days, and it was one of the most unforgettable experiences of my life. The city is lovely and quaint, and I would suggest it to anybody searching for a real Italian experience.

FAQ

You may have concerns about what to anticipate as a tourist to this attractive Italian city, where to go, and how to make the most of your stay here. To assist you, we have created a list of commonly asked questions (FAQ) that will offer you all of the information you want for an unforgettable stay in Lucca.

Where exactly is Lucca?

Lucca is located in the Tuscany region of central Italy. It lies 80 kilometers west of Florence and 20 km east of Pisa.

How do I get to Lucca?

Lucca is easily accessible by rail, bus, and vehicle. Pisa International Airport (Galileo Galilei) and Florence Airport (Amerigo Vespucci) are the nearest airports. You may easily reach Lucca by rail or bus from there.

When is the best time of year to visit Lucca?

Lucca is open all year, but the ideal seasons to visit are spring (April to June) and autumn (September to October) when the weather is good and the city is less congested. If you don't mind crowds, the summer months (July and August) provide a bustling environment with a variety of events and festivals.

What are the must-see sights in Lucca?

Lucca is famous for its well-preserved Renaissance walls, which may be walked or cycled along for panoramic city views. The Cathedral of San Martino, Guinigi Tower, Piazza dell'Anfiteatro, and the Basilica of San Frediano are among must-sees.

Is it possible to hire a bike in Lucca?

Yes, renting a bike is a popular method to see the sights of Lucca. Near the city walls, there are various rental businesses where you may hire bicycles for a few hours or a full day. Cycling around town is a pleasurable activity that enables you to cover more territory in less time.

Are there any day trips from Lucca?

Yes, Lucca is a fantastic starting point for day visits to other gorgeous Tuscany places. You may go to Pisa to view the famed Leaning Tower, Florence to experience its rich art and culture, or the Cinque Terre seaside area.

What is the native food in Lucca like?

Lucca offers a wonderful selection of Tuscan food. Don't miss out on trying local delicacies like "buccellato" (raisin and anise sweet bread), *"tordelli lucchesi"* (stuffed pasta), and *"cecina"* (a chickpea flour pancake). Pair your lunch with a glass of local wine, such as one of Tuscany's well-known reds.

Are there any festivals or events in Lucca?

Throughout the year, Lucca holds several festivals and events. The Lucca Summer Festival, which draws globally renowned performers to the city for a series of performances, is one of the most well-known. Lucca Comics & Games is also a major event for comic book and gaming fans.

Is Lucca a pedestrian-friendly city?

Yes, Lucca is well-known for its walkable streets. The historic center is mainly car-free, enabling tourists to explore the city on foot and avoid traffic. As a result, it is a pleasant and secure place for strolls.

In Lucca, where can I get tourist information?

The major tourist information office is situated in the city's main plaza, Piazza Napoleone. Maps, brochures, and friendly personnel may be found here, as well as extra information and support.

In Lucca, where should I stay?

There are plenty of excellent places to stay in Lucca, ranging from inexpensive hostels to elegant hotels. Consider lodging in the historic district if you want to be centrally located. If you want to remain beyond the city walls, Lucca is close to numerous attractive villages and towns.

What should I bring with me to Lucca?

Pack suitable walking shoes since you will be walking a lot in Lucca. For the warmer months, you should also bring a hat and sunscreen. If you want to attend any churches, bring some modest apparel with you.

What are the customs of Lucca?

The people of Lucca are kind and friendly. Remember to say *"buongiorno"* (good morning) or *"buonasera"* (good evening) to them. It is normal to leave a little gratuity while eating in a restaurant.

What are some of the most popular scams to avoid in Lucca?

Pickpockets should be avoided, particularly in busy places. Keep your valuables close at hand at all times. In Lucca, there have also been allegations of phony tour guides. Make certain that you schedule your trips with a reliable provider.

11

What is the cost of traveling to Lucca?

- The cost of traveling to Lucca depends on your budget. The following is a preliminary estimation of the costs:
- Flights: Flights from major US locations to Pisa airport start at roughly $100.
- Trains: Prices for trains from Florence to Lucca start at about $10.
- Bus: Prices for buses from Pisa to Lucca start at $5.
- Accommodation in Lucca starts at around $20 per night. Lucca hotels start at about $50 per night.
- Food: Food in Lucca is reasonably priced. An excellent supper will cost you roughly $10.
- Activities: Activities in Lucca are also reasonably priced. The majority of the city's attractions are free to see.

Key Fact About Lucca

Lucca is a lovely Italian city in the Tuscany area. Lucca has become a famous tourist destination for visitors from all over the globe due to its rich history, breathtaking architecture, and dynamic culture. *Here are some interesting facts about Lucca that make it a must-see destination:*

Historical Importance: Lucca has a long history dating back to ancient Roman times. The Etruscans established it, and it afterward became a Roman colony. Lucca has been dominated by numerous forces throughout the years, notably the Lombards, the Franks, and the Republic of Pisa. The well-preserved city walls, which were erected in the 16th century and still ring the city today, attest to its historical importance.

City Walls: Lucca is notable for its well-preserved city walls, which are one of Europe's best-preserved examples of Renaissance fortifications. The walls are around 4.2 km long and large enough to support a tree-lined promenade on top.

Visitors may ride bicycles or wander around the walls at their leisure, taking in panoramic views of the city and its surroundings.

Architectural Marvels: Lucca is home to a plethora of architectural wonders that exhibit its rich history and cultural heritage. The church of San Martino, a majestic Romanesque-Gothic church that holds the famed Volto Santo, a wooden crucifix said to have been carved by Nicodemus, one of Jesus' followers, is one of the most prominent sights. The Guinigi Tower, which is crowned with oak trees, and the Piazza dell'Anfiteatro, a distinctive oval-shaped plaza constructed on the remnants of an old Roman amphitheater, are other significant architectural marvels.

Music & Culture: Lucca has a rich musical legacy and is notable for being the home of the legendary composer Giacomo Puccini. Lucca Summer event, an annual music event held in the city, draws well-known worldwide performers and bands. Lucca also has several museums, art galleries, and theatres, allowing tourists to immerse themselves in the city's thriving cultural environment.

Culinary Delights: Lucca is a foodie's heaven, with a diverse selection of gastronomic pleasures. Traditional Tuscan cuisine includes meals such as ribollita (a hearty vegetable soup), bistecca alla Fiorentina (Florentine-style steak), and torta di riso (rice cake). Lucca is particularly well-known for its olive oil and wine production, and the surrounding area is dotted with vineyards and olive trees.

Festivals & Events: Throughout the year, Lucca stages many festivals and events that contribute to the city's dynamic atmosphere. The Lucca Comics & Games, Europe's biggest comic book and gaming convention, is one of the most popular events. Thousands of fans attend this event to view the newest comics, meet their favorite creators, and compete in costume contests. The Lucca Summer Festival, the Lucca Film Festival, and the Lucca Antiques Market are all significant events.

Bicycling heaven: With its flat topography and well-maintained riding trails, Lucca is a cyclist's heaven. Bicycles are a popular means of transportation for both residents and tourists since they enable visitors to explore the city at their leisure. It is simple to hire a bike, and there are various rental businesses located around the city. Cycling through the city walls or across the gorgeous countryside is an excellent way to appreciate Lucca's splendor.

To summarize, Lucca is a city that combines history, culture, and natural beauty. The city offers something for everyone, from its well-preserved city walls to its architectural wonders. Whether you're a history buff, a music lover, a foodie, or just want to immerse yourself in the Italian way of life, Lucca is a must-see location. Let's delve in and explore!

Lucca Travel Planner

Date: _____

Destination: _____

Address: _____ Transportation: _____

What To Do	Location
--------------------------------	------------------
--------------------------------	------------------
--------------------------------	------------------
--------------------------------	------------------
--------------------------------	------------------
--------------------------------	------------------
--------------------------------	------------------
--------------------------------	------------------
--------------------------------	------------------

Note: _____

_____

_____

CHAPTER 1

Discovering Lucca: A Charming Italian Gem

L ucca is a hidden treasure that captivates everyone who comes. From its well-preserved medieval walls to its picturesque cobblestone lanes, this city provides travelers seeking a genuine Italian trip with a one-of-a-kind and memorable experience. The most distinguishing feature of Lucca is its surviving Renaissance-era walls, which enclose the whole city.

These walls, which were originally created as a protective barrier, today serve as a magnificent promenade with panoramic views of the city and its surroundings. Walking or cycling up the tree-lined walls is a must-do activity for any tourist looking for a peaceful respite from the hectic streets below. When you enter the city gates, you will be transported back in time.

The ancient center of Lucca is a maze of winding alleyways studded with beautiful castles, medieval turrets, and attractive piazzas. The Torre Guinigi, a tower with old oak trees at its peak, is one of the city's most recognizable sights. Climbing to the peak provides amazing views of the town and neighboring Tuscan countryside.

Lucca is also known for its beautiful churches. With its complex façade and gorgeous marble interior, the Cathedral of San Martino is a monument to the city's rich ecclesiastical tradition. The Basilica of San Frediano, with its remarkable mosaic façade and exquisite Romanesque architecture, is another renowned church. Exploring these hallowed locations provides insight into Lucca's spiritual background as well as the creative expertise of its artisans. Lucca is a cultural treasure trove for art connoisseurs. Several museums and galleries in the city display work by well-known Italian painters. A huge collection of paintings, sculptures, and ornamental art may be seen in the Palazzo Mansi, a magnificent 16th-century mansion.

Another must-see is the Museo Nazionale di Palazzo Guinigi, which has an amazing collection of medieval and Renaissance art. Lucca's strong cultural landscape is not limited to its museums. Throughout the year, the city conducts a number of festivals and events to commemorate its rich legacy and customs. The Lucca Summer Festival, which draws world-class musicians and entertainers to its ancient venues, is one of the most well-known.

The streets come alive during the Lucca Comics & Games festival when fans of comic books, animation, and gaming join together to celebrate their interests. No trip to Lucca would be complete without sampling the city's gastronomic offerings. The city is well-known for its traditional Tuscan cuisine, which features simple but tasty meals. Lucca provides a gourmet experience that will tickle your taste buds, from robust soups and luscious roasted meats to exquisite pastries and gelato. Don't forget to have a bottle of local wine with your lunch, since Tuscany is known for its vineyards and world-class vintages.

Lucca is bordered by scenic scenery, studded with vineyards, olive groves, and attractive hilltop towns, outside the municipal boundaries. You may explore the gorgeous Tuscan environment at your own leisure by renting a bicycle or a vehicle. A short drive from Lucca takes you to the renowned Leaning Tower of Pisa or the stunning Cinque Terre, a UNESCO World Heritage site noted for its colorful cliffside towns.

Finally, Lucca is a delightful Italian jewel that provides tourists with a one-of-a-kind and genuine experience. It is a must-see site in Tuscany because of its well-preserved medieval walls, historic center, and cultural attractions. Lucca will make an indelible stamp on your heart and create memories that will last a lifetime, whether you're wandering along the walls, admiring the art in its museums, or savoring the local food.

Unveiling the Allure of Lucca

Lucca's well-preserved medieval walls, which surround the whole city, are one of its most outstanding characteristics. These centuries-old defense walls today serve as a unique promenade, allowing tourists to take leisurely walks or bike rides while enjoying panoramic views of the city and its surroundings. The tranquillity and beauty of this elevated promenade give a feeling of calm and an opportunity to observe the city from a new viewpoint.

Going into the medieval center of Lucca is like going back in time. The cobblestone lanes of the city, flanked by stately palaces, old towers, and attractive piazzas, create a timeless beauty. Exploring the city's small passageways and secret nooks exposes a treasure trove of architectural marvels. The Torre Guinigi, with its stately oak trees on top, is a symbol of Lucca's rich history and provides beautiful views of the metropolis.

With its elaborate façade and awe-inspiring interior, the Cathedral of San Martino exemplifies the city's ecclesiastical legacy as well as its creative brilliance. Art fans will discover Lucca to be a cultural sanctuary. The city is home to various museums and galleries that showcase remarkable art collections. The Palazzo Mansi, a 16th-century magnificent mansion, has a diverse collection of paintings, sculptures, and decorative arts. Another must-see attraction is the Museo Nazionale di Palazzo Guinigi, which has an impressive collection of medieval and Renaissance art. These cultural institutions provide an insight into Lucca's creative legacy as well as the skill of its famous Italian painters.

Lucca's strong cultural landscape is not limited to its museums. Throughout the year, the city stages a number of festivals and events to celebrate its traditions and bring the streets to life. The Lucca Summer Festival draws world-class artists and performers to its ancient locations, where they provide memorable live music experiences. The Lucca Comics & Games Festival, on the other hand, brings together fans of comics, animation, and gaming, resulting in a dynamic and colorful ambiance that is really one-of-a-kind.

No trip to Lucca would be complete without sampling the city's gastronomic offerings. The city is well-known for its traditional Tuscan cuisine, which focuses on simple but tasty meals produced from fresh, local ingredients. Lucca's gourmet offerings range from substantial soups and delectable roasted meats to exquisite pastries and gelato. The gastronomic trip is enhanced further by pairing these delightful delicacies with a glass of local wine since Tuscany is famed for its great vineyards and world-class vintages.

Lucca is surrounded by gorgeous landscape, studded with vineyards, olive groves, and lovely hilltop towns, outside the municipal boundaries. Exploring the Tuscan countryside is a must-do activity for nature lovers and thrill-seekers alike. Visitors may explore the scenic countryside by renting a bicycle or a vehicle, where they can find hidden jewels such as the Leaning Tower of Pisa or the breathtaking Cinque Terre, a collection of colorful cliffside towns that have grabbed the hearts of travelers from all over the globe.

Finally, Lucca is a city that reveals its charm to those who visit it. Lucca provides a really wonderful experience that encapsulates the soul of Italy, with its well-preserved walls, medieval center, cultural attractions, and gastronomic pleasures. Lucca will leave an indelible stamp on your spirit and create memories that will last a lifetime, whether you are wandering along the walls, immersing yourself in the city's art and history, or savoring the flavors of Tuscan food.

A Brief History of Lucca

Lucca's history begins with the Etruscans, who built the city in the 7th century BC. In 180 BC, the Romans seized Lucca and established a colony there. During the Roman Empire, Lucca became an important center of trade and commerce. Lucca was governed by a series of Germanic tribes after the collapse of the Roman Empire, including the Goths, Byzantines, and Lombards. Lucca joined the Holy Roman Empire in the ninth century.

Lucca became an autonomous commune in the 11th century. During this time, the city thrived due to its silk manufacturing and commerce with the Islamic world. Lucca also became a cultural and educational center. The Guinigi family controlled Lucca in the 14th century. The Guinigis supported the arts and sciences, and they contributed to establishing Lucca as a center of Renaissance culture.

The Medici dynasty of Florence controlled Lucca in the 16th century. The Medicis did not promote Lucca's independence as much as the Guinigis did, and they finally lost control of the city. Lucca was controlled by a series of dukes in the 18th century. Elisa Bonaparte Baciocchi, Napoleon Bonaparte's sister, was the last Duke of Lucca. Lucca was acquired by the Grand Duchy of Tuscany in 1847. Lucca joined the Kingdom of Italy in 1860. Since then, the city has been a part of Italy. Lucca is a lovely medieval city with a rich cultural and historical heritage. It is a renowned tourist attraction as well as the location of many institutions and colleges.

Lucca is a lively and interesting city that is a wonderful location to live, work, and visit.

Here are some significant events in Lucca's history:

- The Etruscans discovered Lucca around the seventh century BC.
- 180 BC: The Romans take Lucca and establish a colony there.
- The Roman Empire falls in 476 AD. A series of Germanic tribes control Lucca.
- Lucca joins the Holy Roman Empire in the ninth century.
- Lucca becomes an autonomous commune in the 11th century.
- The Guinigi family rules Lucca in the 14th century.
- The Medici dynasty of Florence rules over Lucca in the 16th century.
- Lucca is controlled by a line of dukes, notably Elisa Bonaparte Baciocchi in the 18th century.

- The Grand Duchy of Tuscany annexes Lucca in 1847.
- Lucca joins the Kingdom of Italy in 1860.

Nowadays, Lucca is a major tourist destination and a thriving city with a rich cultural and traditional heritage.

People and Culture

Lucca is a lovely city in Tuscany, Italy. It is well-known for its well-preserved medieval walls, many churches, and vibrant culture. The inhabitants of Lucca are famed for their friendliness and hospitality, and they are always eager to greet guests. *Here's a deeper look at Lucca's people and culture:*

The Lucca People

Lucca's population is a mix of Italians from all over the nation as well as individuals from other countries who have chosen to live in Lucca because of its beauty and charm.

The inhabitants of Lucca are famed for their friendliness and hospitality, and they are always eager to greet guests. One of the things that distinguishes the inhabitants of Lucca is their passion for music. Many notable composers, like Giacomo Puccini, were born in Lucca, and the city maintains a thriving music culture. Throughout the year, there are concerts and opera performances, and the people of Lucca are always ready for a good time. Another characteristic that distinguishes the residents of Lucca is their love of cuisine. Lucca is home to some of Tuscany's top restaurants, and the people of Lucca know how to eat well. There are several classic Tuscan foods to sample, as well as cosmopolitan fare.

The Lucca Culture

Lucca's culture is a blend of medieval and Renaissance elements. The medieval walls of the city serve as a reminder of its history, while the city's many churches and palaces showcase its Renaissance tradition.

Walking or biking around the city walls is one of the most popular activities to do in Lucca. The walls are about 4 km long and provide breathtaking views of the city. Along the walls, there are several gates and turrets worth investigating. Another favorite pastime in Lucca is visiting the city's many churches. Lucca has over a hundred churches, each with its distinct history and architecture. The Duomo, San Michele in Foro, and the Guinigi Chapel are among Lucca's most prominent churches. There are many museums in Lucca, including the National Museum of Palazzo Mansi, the National Museum of Villa Guinigi, and the Puccini Museum. In Lucca, there are also numerous art galleries and stores where you may buy typical Tuscan souvenirs and presents.

Lucca is a lovely city with a fascinating history and culture. Lucca's residents are kind and inviting, and they are always eager to show tourists around their city. Lucca has a lot to offer, from touring the ancient walls to visiting its various churches and museums.

If you're seeking a pleasant and memorable Italian city to visit, Lucca is the place to go.

Must-Know Travel Tips for a Memorable Stay

- Do your homework. Take some time before you arrive to study Lucca's history, culture, and attractions. This will assist you in making the most of your vacation.
- Bring comfortable shoes. You'll be doing a lot of walking in Lucca, so bring comfortable shoes you can wear all day.
- Purchase a city pass. In Lucca, there are many different city permits available that might save you money on entrance to sights and excursions.
- Stay inside the city limits. If possible, attempt to remain inside the city walls. This gives you quick access to all of the main sites and makes getting around simpler.

- On foot, explore the city. Walking is the greatest way to see Lucca. Take your time exploring the city's small alleys and lanes, and be sure to stop at one of the numerous piazzas.
- Pay a visit to the Piazza dell'Anfiteatro. This lovely square was once home to a Roman amphitheater and is now one of Lucca's most renowned tourist attractions.
- Ascend the Torre Guinigi. Climb the Torre Guinigi for spectacular views of the city. One of Lucca's most recognizable sights is this 44-meter-tall tower.
- See the Lucca Cathedral. This stunning cathedral is one of the most prominent ecclesiastical structures in Lucca.
- Visit the Puccini Museum. This museum is devoted to the life and work of Giacomo Puccini, the famed Italian opera composer.
- Attend a culinary lesson. A local chef will teach you how to cook classic Tuscan cuisine.

- Take advantage of the local food. Lucca has numerous wonderful restaurants that serve traditional Tuscan cuisine.

- Enjoy an aperitivo. Aperitivo is a pre-dinner drink and snack in Italy. It's a terrific opportunity to meet new people while eating amazing meals.

- Take a stroll around the city walls. Lucca's city walls are a UNESCO World Heritage Site. They are well-preserved and provide spectacular views of the city.

- In the parks, you can unwind. Lucca offers numerous lovely parks that are ideal for a quiet day.

- Visit Pisa for the day. Pisa, which is just a short drive from Lucca, is famous for the Leaning Tower of Pisa.

- These are just a handful of the various activities available in Lucca. Lucca is the ideal spot to spend a weekend or longer, with its picturesque streets, rich history, and wonderful cuisine.

Here are some more travel suggestions for a safe and happy stay in Lucca:

- Be mindful of your surroundings and take efforts to avoid being robbed.
- Don't leave anything important unattended.
- Avoid drinking tap water and instead go for bottled water.
- Be considerate of local customs and traditions.
- Learn some fundamental Italian phrases.

With these suggestions in mind, you'll enjoy a wonderful visit to Lucca.

Lucca Travel Planner

Date: _____

Destination: _____

Address: _____ Transportation: _____

What To Do	Location
-------------------------------	-------------------
-------------------------------	-------------------
-------------------------------	-------------------
-------------------------------	-------------------
-------------------------------	-------------------
-------------------------------	-------------------
-------------------------------	-------------------
-------------------------------	-------------------

Note: _____
_____
_____

CHAPTER 2

Best Time to Visit

If you're thinking of visiting Lucca, you may be wondering when the ideal time to go is. In this post, we will look at the many seasons and events in Lucca to help you determine when to come.

Spring (March to May): Lucca comes alive with brilliant colors and nice weather throughout the spring season. Temperatures range from 10 to 20 degrees Celsius (50 to 68 degrees Fahrenheit) throughout this season, making it ideal for exploring the city on foot or by bicycle. The city's parks and gardens are in full bloom, making for a beautiful backdrop for leisurely strolls. Furthermore, spring is when Lucca holds a number of cultural events that draw people from all over the globe, such as the Lucca Film Festival and the Lucca Comics & Games convention.

Summer (June to August): Lucca's summers are warm, with highs ranging from 25 to 30 degrees Celsius (77 to 86 degrees Fahrenheit). This is peak tourist season, with many people flocking to Lucca to enjoy the sun and outdoor activities. During this period, the city's historic center may get congested, particularly in July and August, when many Europeans vacation. Summer, on the other hand, is a terrific season to visit Lucca because of the bustling atmosphere, open-air concerts, and festivals. In July, the Lucca Summer Festival gathers famous worldwide performers to perform in the city's medieval squares.

Autumn (September to November): Autumn is a great season to visit Lucca since the weather is still beautiful and the city is less busy than in the summer. Temperatures begin to fall, ranging from 15 to 25 degrees Celsius (59 to 77 degrees Fahrenheit), offering a pleasant climate in which to explore the city's attractions. Autumn is also harvest season in Tuscany, so you may enjoy the region's gastronomic delicacies like truffles, chestnuts, and new wine. every addition, every

September, Lucca organizes the Lucca Jazz Donna festival, which honors women in jazz and draws renowned performers from all over the globe.

From December until February: The winter months in Lucca are colder, with highs ranging from 8 to 14 degrees Celsius (46 to 57 degrees Fahrenheit). While the city sees fewer visitors during this season, it preserves its beauty and provides a one-of-a-kind experience. The streets are decorated for the holidays, and the Christmas markets create a lovely ambiance. If you like classical music, winter is a wonderful season to visit Lucca since the city organizes the Lucca Winter Festival, which features famous orchestras and performers.

Finally, Lucca is a city that can be experienced throughout the year, with each season bringing its own distinct beauty. Summer is good for individuals who appreciate a vibrant environment and outdoor activities, while spring and fall are ideal for those who prefer warmer weather and wish to avoid crowds. Winter, despite its colder temperatures, provides a spectacular experience with its festive ambiance and cultural activities. Finally, the optimum time to visit Lucca is determined by your particular interests and the sort of experience you are looking for.

Here are some more suggestions for arranging your vacation to Lucca:

- Book your lodgings as soon as possible, particularly if you are traveling during the high season.
- If you want to come during a festival, organize your travel and lodgings ahead of time.
- Wear comfy shoes since you will be walking a lot.
- Even in the spring and autumn, bring a hat and sunscreen.
- Learn a few basic Italian words to help you navigate the city and converse with the people.
- Try the native food, which includes pasta, pizza, and gelato.

- Take some time to unwind and appreciate the lovely city of Lucca.

How to Reach Lucca

If you're considering a vacation to this wonderful city, you should be aware of the many modes of transportation accessible to get to Lucca. In this guide, we will look at the many methods to get to Lucca, ensuring that every guest has a pleasant and interesting voyage.

By Air: Flying into one of the neighboring airports is the most convenient method to get to Lucca from abroad. Pisa International Airport (Galileo Galilei Airport) is the nearest international airport, situated just 18 km from Lucca. You may easily reach Lucca by rail, bus, or taxi from the airport. Florence Airport (Peretola Airport) is another alternative, located around 80 km from Lucca. You can get to Lucca by rail or bus from Florence.

By Train: Due to Italy's effective rail network, travelers often choose to go by train. Lucca Centrale, the city's railway station, is well-connected to major Italian cities. If you're coming from Florence, you may take a direct train to Lucca, which takes around an hour. There are regular trains from Pisa to Lucca that take around 30 minutes. The railway station is within walking distance of the city center of Lucca, making it a handy alternative for tourists.

By Bus: Another inexpensive and convenient means of getting to Lucca is the bus. Several bus companies provide trips to and from Lucca, linking it to other cities and villages. From Pisa, take a bus from the Pisa Airport or the Pisa Central Station, which takes around 30 minutes. There are other buses from Florence that provide a picturesque ride across the Tuscan countryside. Renting a vehicle is a reasonable choice if you want the freedom of driving. Lucca is readily accessible by car since it is well-connected to the Italian motorway network. The A11 roadway connects Pisa to Lucca in roughly 30 minutes.

Take the A11 or A12 motorway from Florence; the trip will take around 1.5 hours. It's worth noting that the old city center of Lucca is mainly pedestrianized, so parking outside the walls and touring on foot is advised.

Thanks to its excellent transit links, getting to Lucca is a simple and delightful experience. Whether you fly into one of the neighboring airports, take the train, bus, or drive, you'll soon be immersed in the fascinating beauty of Lucca. Every tourist will be greeted by the city's rich history, breathtaking architecture, and genuine friendliness. So pack your luggage, organize your trip, and prepare to discover the charming city of Lucca.

Here are several directions to Lucca:

- If you want to travel by rail, get your tickets in advance, particularly if you intend to go during peak season.
- If you're taking the bus, it's a good idea to check the bus schedule ahead of time so you can organize your trip.

- If you are driving to Lucca, make sure you have a decent city map. The roads might be difficult to navigate, particularly if you are unfamiliar with the region.
- If you're flying into Lucca, look out for taxi and bus schedules ahead of time so you can organize your trip.

Transportation: Getting Around with Ease

Transportation by Public

Vai Bus is the principal public transportation operator in Lucca. They manage a bus fleet that travels around the city and to some of the outlying districts. If you don't want to walk or have a lot of baggage, buses are an excellent method to travel to Lucca. Single bus tickets are priced at €1.50. A day ticket costs €4.50, while a three-day pass costs €12.00. Tickets are available from the bus driver as well as cigarette stores and newsstands.

Trains

Trains serve Lucca as well. The railway station lies just outside the municipal limits. Trains link Lucca to other Tuscan towns as well as Florence and Pisa. A single rail ticket costs €1.60. A day ticket costs €9.00, while a three-day pass costs €21.00. Tickets are available at the railway station, as well as cigarette stores and newsstands.

Taxis

Taxis are available in Lucca, however, they are not always essential for moving about. Taxis may be costly, therefore they should only be used for longer travels or to go to and from the railway station or bus terminal. In Lucca, the standard cost for a cab is €3.00. The meter is used to compute fares, and there is an extra fee for bags.

Bicycles

Bicycles are an excellent mode of transportation in Lucca. The city is rather level, and there are several bike lanes. Bicycles may be rented from a number of stores in the city center.

Renting a bicycle costs around €10.00 per day. You must provide a deposit, which will be repaid once the bicycle is returned.

Walking

Walking is the greatest way to see Lucca. The city walls are totally walkable, and the city center has several pedestrian-only streets. Walking is a terrific way to get some exercise while also getting to know the city at a slower pace.

Here is a rundown of the transit choices in Lucca:

- Vai Bus maintains a bus fleet that travels around the city and to some of the neighboring districts. Single bus tickets are priced at €1.50. A day ticket costs €4.50, while a three-day pass costs €12.00.
- Train: Trains service Lucca as well. The railway station lies just outside the municipal limits. Trains link Lucca to other Tuscan towns as well as Florence and Pisa. A single rail ticket costs

€1.60. A day ticket costs €9.00, while a three-day pass costs €21.00.

- Taxis are available in Lucca, however, they are not always essential for moving about. Taxis may be costly, therefore they should only be used for longer travels or to go to and from the railway station or bus terminal. In Lucca, the standard cost for a cab is €3.00. The meter is used to compute fares, and there is an extra fee for bags.

- Bicycles: Bicycles are an excellent mode of transportation in Lucca. The city is rather level, and there are several bike lanes. Bicycles may be rented from a number of stores in the city center. Renting a bicycle costs around €10.00 per day. You must provide a deposit, which will be repaid once the bicycle is returned.

- Walking: Walking is the greatest way to see Lucca. The city walls are totally walkable, and the city center has several pedestrian-only streets. Walking is a terrific way to get some exercise while also getting to know the city at a slower pace.

Accommodation Options

Lucca offers something to meet any traveler's requirements and interests, whether they are seeking luxurious hotels, comfortable bed and breakfasts, or budget-friendly hostels. In this post, we will look at the numerous hotel alternatives in Lucca, as well as their rates, to help you plan your visit to this lovely city.

Luxury Hotels: Lucca is home to various luxury hotels that provide first-rate facilities and services to discriminating travelers. The Grand Hotel Guinigi, situated in Lucca's old center, is one such hotel. This five-star hotel has luxuriously appointed rooms, a spa, a rooftop terrace with panoramic views, and a gourmet restaurant. A twin room at the Grand Hotel Guinigi costs roughly **€300** per night. The Hotel Noblesse, a boutique hotel set in a historic structure, is another luxurious alternative. The hotel has elegantly designed rooms, a bar, a garden, and a spa center. A double room at Hotel Noblesse costs between **€250** and **€400** per night, depending on the season.

Mid-Range Hotels: If you're seeking pleasant lodging at a lower cost, Lucca offers a number of mid-range hotels to select from. Visitors often choose the Hotel Ilaria & Residenza dell'Alba. This hotel within the city walls has big rooms, a courtyard, a bar, and a daily breakfast. A twin room at Hotel Ilaria & Residenza dell'Alba costs around **€150** per night. The Hotel Alla Corte degli Angeli, a lovely hotel located in a refurbished 17th-century structure, is another alternative. The hotel has distinctively furnished rooms as well as a garden and a bar. A double room at Hotel Alla Corte degli Angeli costs between **€120** and **€200** per night.

Bed & Breakfasts: Consider staying at one of Lucca's bed and breakfasts for a more private and comfortable experience. B&Bs provide a homey environment as well as individual service. La Romea Residenza d'Epoca is an excellent B&B in a historic property. It has tastefully equipped rooms, a garden, and free breakfast. A twin room at La Romea Residenza d'Epoca costs roughly **€100** per night.

48

The B&B Antica Residenza dell'Angelo, located in a 17th-century structure, is another popular option. This bed and breakfast offers pleasant rooms, a patio, and a breakfast buffet. A double room at B&B Antica Residenza dell'Angelo costs between €80 and €120 per night.

Hostels: For budget-conscious travelers, Lucca offers a few hostels that provide economical lodging without sacrificing comfort. Ostello San Frediano is a strategically situated hostel with both a dormitory and private rooms. There is a shared kitchen, a lounge, and a bar. A bed in a dormitory room at Ostello San Frediano costs around €20 per night. The Lucca in Villa Elisa & Gentucca hostel, situated in a quiet residential neighborhood, is another choice. This hostel has dorm rooms, private rooms, a garden, and a communal kitchen. A bed in a dormitory room at Villa Elisa & Gentucca in Lucca costs between €15 and €30 per night.

Finally, Lucca offers a variety of hotel alternatives to meet any traveler's budget and interests. There is something for everyone, from luxurious hotels to charming bed & breakfasts and budget-friendly hostels. rates vary based on the kind of accommodation and the season, so it's better to book ahead of time and check rates to get the best bargain for your Lucca visit.

Budgeting and Costs

To make the most of your vacation as a guest, you must carefully manage your money. In this article, we will look at budgeting and costs in Lucca, such as lodging, transportation, food, attractions, and incidental charges.

Accommodation: Lucca has a variety of lodging alternatives to suit all budgets. There is something for everyone, from luxury hotels to budget-friendly hostels and vacation rentals. A mid-range hotel room in Lucca may cost between €80 and €120 per night, while budget choices like Italian hostels or guesthouses can be obtained for as little as €30 to €50 per night.

Apartments and villas for rent are also popular, with prices ranging from €60 to €150 a night depending on location and amenities.

Transportation: Getting to Lucca is pretty simple since it is well-served by a variety of modes of transportation. If you arrive by plane, the closest international airport is Pisa International Airport, which is just 20 km away. You may get to Lucca by rail, bus, or taxi from the airport. The railway is the most convenient and affordable alternative, with tickets ranging from €5 to €10 depending on class and time of departure.

The city of Lucca is best visited on foot or by bicycle. The ancient center of Lucca is surrounded by well-preserved Renaissance-era walls. Bicycles may be hired for around €10-€15 per day and will enable you to explore the city at your own leisure. Buses and other forms of public transit are also available, with tickets costing roughly €1.50 for each journey.

Food: Italian food is world-renowned, and Lucca has a wealth of eating alternatives to suit your palate. There is something for every palette and budget, from classic trattorias to sophisticated restaurants and lovely cafés. A typical lunch at a mid-range restaurant may be between €15 and €25 per person, not including drinks. For a more affordable choice, consider street food or a piece of pizza for roughly €5-€8. Furthermore, Lucca is well-known for its gelato, with a scoop costing as little as €2.

Attractions: Lucca is a historic city with a plethora of sights worth seeing. The most recognizable feature of the city is its surviving Renaissance walls, which provide panoramic views of the city. Walking or cycling along the walls is free and offers a unique view of Lucca's splendor. Lucca also has various churches, including the Cathedral of San Martino and the Basilica of San Frediano, which may be visited for a modest cost of roughly €3-€5.

The Lucca Centre of Contemporary Art (Lu. C.C.A) is a must-see for art lovers. The museum exhibits modern art and often holds temporary exhibitions. The entry charge ranges between €8 and €10. The Guinigi Tower, with its rooftop garden, is another famous destination. Climbing the tower costs around €4-€6 and provides spectacular views of the city.

Miscellaneous costs: It is important to budget for miscellaneous costs like as souvenirs, shopping, and entertainment while visiting Lucca. Lucca is well-known for its local markets, where you can purchase one-of-a-kind handicrafts, apparel, and vegetables. Prices vary based on the item, but budget between €50 and €100 for shopping. Ticket fees for events or concerts may vary from €10 to €50, depending on the location and performance. Check the local event calendar to see if any festivals or cultural activities are scheduled during your stay.

Lucca provides guests with a lovely experience, and with careful budgeting, you can make the most of your vacation without breaking the bank. You can efficiently manage your budget by taking into account the prices of lodging, transportation, meals, attractions, and incidental charges. Remember to budget for unforeseen costs and leave some room for impromptu adventures. You can enjoy all Lucca has to offer while remaining within your budget if you prepare ahead of time.

Lucca Travel Planner 🪐

Date: _____

Destination: _____

Address: _____   Transportation: _____

What To Do	Location

Note: _____
_____
_____

CHAPTER 3

Exploring Lucca

The well-preserved Renaissance walls that ring the whole city are one of Lucca's features. Visitors may enjoy the panoramic views of the city and its surroundings by taking a leisurely walk or renting a bicycle. The walls are also ideal for a picnic or a moment of relaxation.

Historic City Walls

The Lucca Historic City Walls are one of Europe's most spectacular and well-preserved Renaissance defenses. They are a UNESCO World Heritage Site and one of Tuscany's most popular tourist destinations. The walls were constructed between 1513 and 1670 to replace older defenses erected by the Romans, Etruscans, and the medieval city-state of Lucca. The new walls were constructed with a broad moat and a succession of bastions to be more effective against cannon.

The walls stretch for 4.2 km and reach a height of 12 meters at their highest point. They are divided into 11 bastions and 6 gates. The gates are named after the saints or holy persons who have been consecrated to them. Walking, jogging, and biking are common activities along the walls. They provide breathtaking views of the city and surrounding countryside. Within the walls, there are also various gardens and parks, making it a wonderful spot to rest and enjoy the outdoors.

In addition to its historical and cultural value, Lucca's walls are vital to the city's economy. Every year, millions of visitors visit, contributing to the local economy by staying in hotels, dining at restaurants, and buying in stores. If you visit Lucca, be sure to spend some time exploring the city walls. They are a distinct and intriguing aspect of the city's history and culture.

Here are some particular activities you may undertake to appreciate Lucca's Historic City Walls:

- Take a stroll or ride your bike along the tops of the walls. This is an excellent method to gain a good perspective of the city and its surroundings.
- Visit one of the gardens or parks inside the city walls. These are wonderful spots to unwind and enjoy the scenery.
- Investigate one of the city's entrances. Each gate is named after a saint or religious person, and each has its own distinct history.
- Pay a visit to the Museum of the Walls. This museum is housed inside the walls and explains the history and building of the walls.

Whatever you do, you will have a great time visiting the Historic City Walls of Lucca. They are genuinely one-of-a-kind and unforgettable experiences.

Here are some other suggestions for visiting Lucca's Historic City Walls:

- The walls are accessible 24 hours a day, seven days a week. However, the ideal times to visit are

58

early in the morning or late in the evening, when the crowds are fewer.

- There are various entrances to the walls, but the most famous is Porta San Giorgio.
- Walking or biking along the tops of the walls is free. The Museum of the Walls, on the other hand, has a fee.
- Wear comfortable shoes since there will be a lot of walking.
- Bring a camera to record the breathtaking views from the top of the walls.

Piazza dell'Anfiteatro

Piazza dell'Anfiteatro is one of Lucca's most beautiful and recognizable squares. It is an oval plaza constructed on the site of a Roman amphitheater from the first century AD. The amphitheater was demolished in the sixth century AD, although its foundations could still be seen in the Middle Ages. Lorenzo Nottolini, an architect, chose to rebuild the amphitheater and transform it into a public plaza in the nineteenth century. He ordered the

59

structures erected on top of the amphitheater destroyed and replaced them with a lovely plaza complete with arched arcades and a central fountain. It's simple to understand why Piazza dell'Anfiteatro is a popular tourist attraction. With its colorful houses and meandering lanes, the plaza is lovely and welcoming. There are several cafés and restaurants on the plaza where you may eat or drink while people-watching. There are typically street performers in the area, so you may listen to live music or see some entertainment. If you want to have an unforgettable time in Lucca, go to Piazza dell'Anfiteatro. It is a very unique location that will linger with you long after you leave.

Here are some of the activities available at Piazza dell'Anfiteatro:

- Take a leisurely walk around the plaza to see the wonderful buildings. Look up at the arches and windows to see if you can locate any of the Roman remains that remain visible.

- Cafes and eateries to visit: In Piazza dell'Anfiteatro, there are several places to dine and drink. Enjoy a meal while overlooking the plaza, or just stop for a coffee or gelato.
- See a street performance: Street performers may often be seen in Piazza dell'Anfiteatro. While people-watching, listen to some live music or see some entertainment.
- Take a photograph: A photographer's fantasy is Piazza dell'Anfiteatro. Take pictures of the plaza and the neighboring buildings.
- Simply relax and enjoy the ambiance: Piazza dell'Anfiteatro is a wonderful spot to unwind and absorb the mood. Sit on a bench and people-watch, or just relax and take in the scenery.

Whatever you do at Piazza dell'Anfiteatro, you will have a fantastic experience. It is a very unique location that is definitely worth a visit.

Here are some more things to do at Piazza dell'Anfiteatro:

- The square is busiest during the summer months, so go in the spring or autumn to escape the crowds.
- The square has four entrances, one at each point of the ellipse.
- The entrance charge to the square is minimal, but well worth it.
- There are lots of parking spots around the plaza, however, they might be difficult to locate during busy hours.
- If you want to dine or drink on the plaza, be sure to have cash. The square is devoid of ATMs.

Duomo di San Martino

The major church of Lucca, Italy, is the Duomo di San Martino. It's a Roman Catholic cathedral honoring Saint Martin of Tours. The cathedral was constructed in the 11th and 12th centuries in a Romanesque and Gothic style. It is one of the most significant architectural sites in Lucca and is regarded as one of Italy's greatest examples of Romanesque architecture. The cathedral is situated on the Piazza San Martino in the center of Lucca. It is a massive and imposing structure with a towering bell tower and a lovely front. The front is composed of white marble and is embellished with sculptures and reliefs. The most well-known is the Labirinto di Lucca, a labyrinth that is claimed to depict life's journey.

The cathedral's interior is equally as stunning as its appearance. With a lofty roof and a succession of side chapels, the nave is long and narrow. The walls and floor are frescoed and painted, and the floor is marble. The Volto Santo, a wooden crucifix thought to have been carved by Nicodemus, is the cathedral's most notable piece of art. The Volto Santo is one of Italy's most revered relics, and it is said to have magical abilities. The Duomo di San Martino is a must-see for every Lucca tourist.

It is a stunning and historic structure rich in art and religious importance. *Here are some recommendations for visiting the cathedral:*

- To avoid crowds, arrive early in the morning.
- Wear comfortable shoes since there will be a lot of walking.
- Take your time admiring the architecture and artwork.
- Be mindful of the cathedral's religious importance.
- The Duomo di San Martino is a wonderfully spectacular structure that will make an indelible impact on any visitor.

Here are a few more facts regarding the cathedral's history and architecture:

- Bishop Anselmo da Baggio, afterward Pope Alexander II, began construction on the church in 1063.
- In 1070, the cathedral was dedicated.

64

- In the 14th and 15th centuries, the cathedral was expanded.

- The front of the cathedral was renovated in the 12th century.

- The campanile of the cathedral was erected in the 12th century.

- Nicodemus is supposed to have crafted the Volto Santo, a wooden crucifix.

- The Volto Santo arrived in Lucca in the ninth century.

- The Volto Santo is one of Italy's most revered religious symbols.

- Jacopo della Quercia created the marble sculpture of Ilaria del Carretto.

- Domenico Ghirlandaio created the fresco The Sacra Conversazione.

- Tintoretto's artwork The Ultima Cena.

The Duomo di San Martino is a magnificent and ancient cathedral that every tourist to Lucca should see. It is a house of worship, a piece of art, and a reminder of the city's long past.

Guinigi Tower

The Guinigi Tower is one of Lucca's most iconic sights. It is a 44-meter-tall tower constructed in the 14th century. The tower is well-known for its tree-planted roof garden. The Guinigi family, one of the most influential families in Lucca during the Middle Ages, erected the Guinigi Tower. The tower was built as a defense tower and afterward turned into a dwelling. Over the ages, the tower has been renovated multiple times, and it is currently available to the public for a price.

The Guinigi Tower is situated in the ancient center of Lucca. It is surrounded by historic structures and small lanes. The tower is easily accessible by foot, and there is a nearby parking lot. Visitors must ascend a spiral staircase to get access to the Guinigi Tower. Although the staircase is tiny and steep, it is not difficult to ascend. Visitors may enjoy spectacular views of Lucca and the surrounding countryside from the top of the tower.

Several huge trees may be seen on the Guinigi Tower's roof garden. The trees are a popular destination for both visitors and residents. Visitors may rest on the roof garden seats and take in the view. The Guinigi Tower is a must-see for every Lucca tourist. It's a wonderful piece of history with beautiful views of the city. The tower is available to the public for a price, and the climb is definitely worth it.

Here are some more facts about the Guinigi Tower:

- The tower is 44 meters (144 feet) high.
- It has nine stories.
- Three big holm oak trees may be seen on the roof garden.
- The tower was constructed in the 14th century.
- Originally, it served as a defense tower.
- It was then turned into a house.
- Over the ages, the tower has been renovated multiple times.
- It is available to the public for a price.

The Guinigi Tower is a famous tourist attraction that may become congested in the summer. If you intend to go, it is advisable to go early in the morning or late in the evening to avoid crowds. Weddings and other gatherings are very popular at the tower. If you want to conduct an event in the tower, you must first contact the city of Lucca for further information.

Basilica of San Frediano

San Frediano Basilica is a Romanesque church in Lucca, Italy. It is one of the city's most notable churches and a major tourist attraction. The church, dedicated to Saint Frediano, the patron saint of Lucca, was erected in the 12th century. The church is famous for its stunning design, which includes an ornate façade and two bell towers. The Basilica of San Frediano's most outstanding feature is its façade. It's composed of white limestone and has a big mosaic of Christ the Redeemer rising to heaven. The mosaic is credited to the Lucca-based Berlinghieri school and is considered one of Italy's most prominent examples of Romanesque mosaic art.

The inside of San Frediano Basilica is very magnificent. It is split into three naves, each with its own colonnade of marble columns. The naves are embellished with paintings and other works of art spanning from the 12th to the 18th century. The 12th-century baptismal font is one of the Basilica of San Frediano's most noteworthy artworks. The font is constructed of marble and is adorned with reliefs illustrating Moses' stories, the Apostles' stories, and the months of the year.

The Chapel of Sant'Agostino is another gem of the Basilica of San Frediano. The chapel is embellished with paintings made in the 1500s by Emilian artist Amico Aspertini. The paintings show incidents from Saint Augustine's life. The Basilica of San Frediano is a historical and aesthetic treasure trove. Anyone interested in Romanesque architecture or Renaissance art should go.

Why should tourists pay the admission fee?

There are various reasons why tourists should pay the San Frediano Basilica admission charge. For starters, the church is a UNESCO World Legacy Site, and its preservation is critical to Italy's cultural legacy. Second, the church has a number of significant artworks, including a mosaic facade from the 12th century and a baptismal font from the same era. Third, the church is a major tourist attraction, and the admission price helps to defray the costs of preserving the building and providing tours and other educational activities.

Here are some of the reasons why you should include a visit to the Basilica of San Frediano in your Lucca itinerary:

- The church is a stunning piece of Romanesque architecture.
- The inside of the church is lavishly adorned with mosaics and frescoes.
- The church has a variety of significant artworks, including a Giotto painting.

- The church is situated in the middle of Lucca, making it easily accessible from the city's other attractions.
- I suggest getting a guided tour if you want to understand more about the Basilica of San Frediano's history and art. There are a variety of trips offered, so you can choose one that suits your interests and budget.

Tips for Visiting San Frediano Basilica

Here are some pointers for visiting San Frediano Basilica:

- Visit early in the morning or late in the afternoon. During certain times, the church is less packed.
- Visit the church for at least an hour. This will provide you ample time to see the major artworks and visit the chapel.
- Wear something modest. Because the church is a place of worship, it is necessary to dress appropriately.

- Respect the other guests as well as the church personnel. Because the church is a holy space, you must be conscious of your behavior.

The following holidays are observed by the church:

- New Year's Day is January 1st.
- Sunday and Monday after Easter
- Labour Day is on May 1st.
- The Assumption of the Virgin Mary is celebrated on August 15th.
- All Saints' Day is celebrated on November 1st.
- Christmas Day is celebrated on December 25th.
- Saint Stephen's Day is celebrated on December 26.

The dress code

The Basilica of San Frediano does not have a rigorous dress code. Visitors, on the other hand, are required to dress respectfully. This implies that shoulders must be covered and shorts must be at least knee length.

Photography

The Basilica of San Frediano allows photography. However, flash photography is prohibited.

Other suggestions for visiting San Frediano Basilica

- Visit the church for at least an hour.
- Wear comfortable shoes since there will be a lot of walking.
- Bring a bottle of water since the church might become heated inside.
- Be mindful of the church's religious essence.
- Climbing on the furnishings or touching the artwork is not permitted.

Follow the staff's directions.

Museo Nazionale di Palazzo Mansi

One of the most prominent art museums in Lucca, Italy, is the Museo Nazionale di Palazzo Mansi. It is located in a stunning Baroque palace that was originally the Mansi family's residence. The museum's collection spans the 16th to 18th century and contains paintings, sculptures, tapestries, and other works of art.

The Mansi family, who were rich silk merchants, erected the palace in the late 16th century. The family commissioned architect Pier Francesco Garzoni to create a palace that reflected their riches and rank. The palace was finished in the early 17th century, and it was lavishly adorned with murals, stuccowork, and tapestries. The Mansi family ran into financial difficulties in the late 18th century, and the palace was sold to the Italian government. In 1965, the government turned the palace into a museum.

74

The museum's collection has a broad range of artworks dating from the 16th to the 18th century. Paintings by Italian painters such as Jacopo Tintoretto, Pietro da Cortona, and Giovanni Battista Tiepolo are among those on display. Sculptures by Italian and Flemish artists such as Giambologna and Jean Boulogne are among those on display. A set of 17th-century Flemish tapestries representing the myth of Jason and the Golden Fleece is among the tapestries on display.

There is also a collection of furniture, ceramics, and other decorative arts in the museum. The furniture comprises items from the Mansi family's personal collection as well as items acquired by the museum throughout time. Porcelain pieces from Chinese, Japanese, and European traditions are included. Anyone interested in art and architecture should visit the Museo Nazionale di Palazzo Mansi. The palace is a stunning example of Baroque architecture, and the museum has some of the best artworks from the 16th to the 18th century.

Here are some more information about the museum that you may find useful:

- The museum is open from 9:00 a.m. to 6:00 p.m., Tuesday through Sunday. Mondays and national holidays are closed.
- Admission is €5 for adults, €3 for reduced rates, and free for children under the age of 18. A combo ticket that includes entrance to the Museo Nazionale di Villa Guinigi is also available for €7.50.
- Getting there: The museum sits in the heart of Lucca, only a few steps from the Piazza del Duomo. The bus stop closest to you is "Piazza Napoleone."
- Wheelchair access is available at the museum. There is an elevator that connects all levels.
- The museum contains a gift store as well as a café. There is also a public library on the premises.

Villa Reale di Marlia

The mansion Reale di Marlia is a 17th-century mansion in Marlia, Italy, just outside of Lucca. It was created as a vacation house for the rich and powerful Medici family. The villa is currently a UNESCO World Heritage Site and may be visited for a charge. The home is surrounded by a vast park separated into many sections. The "Giardino dei Semplici," or Garden of Simples, is the park's most renowned feature. This garden, which was built in the 17th century, comprises around 600 distinct plant species. The Medici family employed the plants in the garden for medical reasons.

Another well-known feature of the park is the *"Casino del Delfino."* This casino was created in the 18th century and was used for amusement by the Medici family. The casino is frescoed and has a variety of rooms that were utilized for various activities such as gambling, dance, and music.

The villa itself is very interesting to visit. It is a vast, opulent structure with a lot of magnificent chambers. The "Sala degli Specchi," or Hall of Mirrors, is the villa's most renowned interior. This mirror-adorned chamber is claimed to be haunted by the spirit of a young lady who died in the villa. The Villa Reale di Marlia is a lovely and historic location. Even if there is an entry price, it is certainly worth the visit.

Here is some more information concerning the Villa Reale di Marlia's visitor fee:

- Adults pay €10
- €5 for children (6-17 years old).
- Children under the age of six: €25 for a free family ticket (2 adults and 2 children).
- Tickets are €7.50 for students, elderly, and individuals with impairments.
- Tickets may be bought online or at the ticket office at the villa. Tuesday through Sunday, from 9 a.m. to 5 p.m.

Here are some recommendations for visiting Villa Reale di Marlia:

- Take your time exploring the villa and the park.
- Wear comfy shoes since you will be walking a lot.
- In the summer, bring sunscreen and a hat since the park may become hot.
- Bring a picnic lunch to eat in the park.
- More information may be found on the villa's website.

CHAPTER 4

Museums and Galleries

Museums and galleries in Lucca provide tourists with a unique chance to learn about the city's history, art, and architecture. In this article, we will look at some of the most renowned museums and galleries that every tourist to Lucca should consider seeing.

Palazzo Pfanner

Palazzo Pfanner is a Baroque mansion in the Italian city of Lucca. The Moriconi family erected it in the 17th century. The Controni family bought the palace in the 18th century and extended and enhanced it. The palace was sold to the Pfanner family in the nineteenth century, who gave it its present name. The palace stands near the city walls in the center of Lucca. It's a big, imposing structure with a central courtyard and a magnificent stairway. Frescoes, stuccowork, and marble adorn the castle.

Palazzo Pfanner's Gardens

Palazzo Pfanner's gardens are one of the most prominent tourist attractions in Lucca. Flowers, fountains, and sculptures abound throughout the grounds. They are a lovely and calm refuge in the middle of the metropolis. The gardens are split into two sections: upper and lower gardens. With geometric flower beds and clipped hedges, the top garden is more formal. The bottom garden is more relaxed, with twisting walks and abundant foliage. The gardens have a number of sculptures, including those of Greek gods and goddesses, as well as those portraying the four seasons. In the center of the grounds, there is also a big fountain.

The Palazzo Pfanner's Interior

The interior of Palazzo Pfanner is available for visits. The receiving hall, which is embellished with murals by Pietro Paolo Scorsini, is the most renowned chamber in the palace. The frescoes portray mythological and historical subjects.

A number of other rooms in the palace are similarly furnished with historical furniture and artwork. The dining room, library, and music room are among these spaces.

The Medical Showcase

Palazzo Pfanner also has a medical display in addition to the grounds and the interior of the palace. The exhibit includes a collection of medical tools and writings belonging to Dr. Pietro Pfanner, a surgeon and the mayor of Lucca in the early twentieth century. The medical display provides an intriguing look into the history of medicine. It is a must-see for anybody interested in medicine or Lucca's history.

Ticket Costs

Admission at Palazzo Pfanner is €5 for adults and €3 for children. There is also a €12 family ticket available. Palazzo Pfanner is open Tuesday through Sunday from 10:00 a.m. to 6:00 p.m. Mondays are off limits.

Visitor Tips for Palazzo Pfanner

- The ideal times to visit Palazzo Pfanner are early in the morning or late in the afternoon when there are fewer people.
- Visit the palace and grounds for at least an hour.
- Wear comfy shoes since you will be walking a lot.
- Bring your camera to capture all of the breathtaking vistas.

National Museum of Villa Guinigi

The Villa Guinigi National Museum is a museum in Lucca, Italy. It is home to a collection of art and artifacts dating from the Middle Ages to the present. The museum is housed in a renovated home erected in the 15th century for the lord of Lucca, Paolo Guinigi. The home is distinguished by its unusual tower, which is topped by a pine tree. The collection of the museum is organized into numerous divisions. The archaeology section contains artifacts discovered during excavations in Lucca and the surrounding region.

The medieval area includes paintings, sculptures, and illuminated manuscripts from the 12th through the 15th centuries. The Renaissance area features paintings by some of the period's most prominent painters, including Botticelli, Ghirlandaio, and Perugino. Works from the 17th and 18th centuries may be found in the Baroque and Neoclassical categories.

The museum also has a musical instrument collection, a library, and an archive. The library has books and manuscripts on a wide range of topics, including art history, archaeology, and musicology. Documents from the Guinigi family's history are housed in the archive. The Villa Guinigi National Museum is a renowned tourist attraction. It is open from 9:00 a.m. to 5:00 p.m. Tuesday through Sunday. Adult admission is €10, seniors' admission is €8, and children's admission is €6.

The collection of the museum is organized into numerous divisions, including:

- Archaeological collection: Artifacts from the Etruscan, Roman, and medieval eras are housed in this area of the museum. A collection of Etruscan bronzes and a Roman mosaic are among the highlights.
- The Renaissance collection includes paintings, sculptures, and other works of art from the 14th through the 17th centuries. Among the highlights are pieces by Fra Angelico, Botticelli, and Ghirlandaio.
- Paintings, sculptures, and other artworks from the 17th to the 19th century are housed in the museum's Baroque and Neoclassical collections. Works by Guercino, Tiepolo, and Canova are among the highlights.
- Religious art collection: From the 14th to the 19th centuries, this area of the museum comprises religious paintings, sculptures, and other artworks. Highlights include a collection of illuminated manuscripts and a Giambologna crucifix.

- Musical instrument collection: The museum's musical instrument collection dates from the 16th to the 19th century. A keyboard by Domenico Scarlatti and a violin by Antonio Stradivari are among the highlights.
- The Villa Guinigi National Museum is a renowned tourist attraction in Lucca. It is open from 9:00 a.m. to 5:00 p.m. Tuesday through Sunday. Adult admission is €10, seniors' admission is €8, and children's admission is €6.

Here are some pointers for visiting the Villa Guinigi National Museum:

- Allow at least two hours to explore the museum.
- Begin your tour with the archaeological collection to get an understanding of Lucca's past.
- Visit the Renaissance collection, which includes some of the museum's most well-known masterpieces.

- Don't miss the religious art collection, which has a number of significant and exquisite paintings and sculptures.
- If you have time, stop by the musical instruments collection to view a wide range of instruments from the 16th to the 19th century.

The National Museum of Villa Guinigi is an excellent venue to learn about Lucca's history and culture. It is a must-see attraction for every tourist in the city.

Puccini Museum

The Puccini Museum in Lucca, Italy, is a must-see for any opera or Italian history enthusiast. The museum is housed in Puccini's boyhood home and displays a collection of the composer's personal possessions, musical instruments, and scores. There are additional exhibitions on the history of opera and Puccini's impact on the genre.

The Birthplace, the Study, and the Exhibition Hall are the three primary areas of the museum. Puccini was born on December 22, 1858, at the Birthplace. Many of Puccini's childhood things, like toys, clothing, and musical instruments, have been restored to their original look in the apartments. A huge collection of pictures and letters documenting Puccini's life and career is also on display.

Many of Puccini's most renowned operas, including La Bohème, Tosca, and Madama Butterfly, were written at The Study. Puccini's desk, piano, and other musical instruments are on display in the room. There are additional book and score racks, as well as a bust of Puccini by sculptor Enrico Caruso.

The Exhibition Hall has a number of exhibitions that look at the history of opera and Puccini's effect on the genre. There are displays on many aspects of opera, such as the text, soundtrack, and staging. Exhibits about Puccini's life and work, as well as his influence on popular culture, are also available.

The Puccini Museum is an intriguing site to learn about one of the greatest opera composers of all time. It is also an excellent site to learn about Italian history and culture.

The Puccini Museum charges the following fees:

- Adults pay €10
- Seniors (65 and older): €8 Students (18-25): €6
- Children (under the age of 18): free Family ticket (two adults and two children): €24
- The museum is open Tuesday through Sunday from 9:00 a.m. to 5:00 p.m. Mondays are off limits.

Here are some more interesting facts regarding the Puccini Museum:

- The museum is situated in the ancient center of Lucca, a lovely Tuscan city.

- On the museum grounds, there is a small café where you may have a coffee or food after your visit.
- The museum is handicapped accessible.
- Audio instructions are available in a variety of languages.

Lucca Travel Planner

Date: _____

Destination: _____

Address: _____ Transportation: _____

What To Do	Location
--------------------------------	--------------------------------
--------------------------------	--------------------------------
--------------------------------	--------------------------------
--------------------------------	--------------------------------
--------------------------------	--------------------------------
--------------------------------	--------------------------------
--------------------------------	--------------------------------
--------------------------------	--------------------------------
--------------------------------	--------------------------------

Note: _____
_____
_____

CHAPTER 5

Lucca for Every Season: Year-round Delights

Spring (March-May): Lucca is beautiful in the spring. The weather is warming up, the flowers are blooming, and the city is bustling with bustle. During the spring, Lucca hosts a number of festivals and events, including the Festa di Santa Zita (April 27th), the Anteprima Vini Della Costa Toscana (April), and the Lucca Classica Music Festival (April-May).

Summer (June-August): Summer is the hottest season in Lucca, but it is also the most popular. There are various outdoor things to enjoy in the city, such as swimming in the Arno River, trekking in the nearby hills, and riding around the old walls. During the summer, Lucca hosts a number of concerts and festivals, including the Lucca Summer Festival (July) and the Lucca Biennale Cartasia (August-September).

Autumn (September-November): Autumn is a lovely season to visit Lucca. The weather is cooling, the leaves are turning color, and the city is still quite calm. During the autumn, Lucca hosts a number of harvest festivals, including the Settembre Lucchese (September) and the Murabilia and Verdemura (September-October).

Winter (December-February): Although winter is the coldest season in Lucca, it is also the most joyful. The city has been decked for Christmas, and there are several Christmas markets and festivities taking place. There are also several options to participate in winter activities such as skiing and snowboarding in the surrounding region.

You will have a lovely time in Lucca no matter what time of year you come. From history and cultural buffs to outdoor enthusiasts and foodies, the city provides something for everyone.

Here are some activities to do in Lucca during each season:

Spring:

- Visit the Giardino Botanico Comunale (Communal Botanical Garden) in the spring to view the magnificent flowers in bloom.
- Enjoy the views of the surrounding countryside while walking or riding your bike around the city walls.
- Attend the Festa di Santa Zita, a celebration celebrating the patron saint of the city.

Summer:

- Swim on the Arno River or one of the city's numerous pools throughout the summer.
- Hike in the nearby hills or ride your bike along the Via Francigena, an old pilgrimage road that runs through Lucca.

Fall:

- Attend a performance or a concert at the Teatro del Giglio.

- Settembre Lucchese, a festival celebrating the city's culture and traditions, takes place in the fall.

- Visit the Lucca Comics and Games Festival, Europe's biggest comic book and gaming event.

- Wine sampling in the nearby region is recommended.

Winter:

- Take advantage of the Christmas markets and other holiday festivities.

- Skate on the ice at Piazza Napoleone.

- Visit the Lucca Winter Festival, which includes concerts, plays, and other activities.

- You will have a lovely time in Lucca no matter what time of year you come. From history and cultural buffs to outdoor enthusiasts and foodies, the city provides something for everyone.

Spring's Blossoming Magic

Lucca is turned into a colorful paradise in the spring. Flowers adorn the city's streets and squares, from the delicate pink petals of cherry blossoms to the vivid yellow blooms of daffodils. The air is filled with the beautiful aroma of flowers, and the trees are filled with the sound of chirping.

In Lucca, there are several spots to admire the spring blooms. The Piazza dell'Anfiteatro is a good spot to start. This lovely area is surrounded by Roman remains and is ideal for relaxing and enjoying the weather. The area is packed with colorful flowers in the spring, and it's a terrific spot to people-watch. The Giardino Botanico Comunale is another fantastic site to see spring blooms. This botanical garden is home to a broad range of plants, including beautiful spring blooms. There are also other greenhouses with plants from throughout the globe.

Take a stroll or ride your bike around the city walls for a more active approach to view the spring blooms. The walls provide spectacular views of the city, and you'll often find people picnicking or sunbathing in the grassy areas around the walls. The spring blooms in Lucca are a wonderfully stunning sight, no matter how you choose to enjoy them. So, if you're planning a vacation to Tuscany in the spring, include Lucca on your schedule.

Here are some extra suggestions for enjoying the Lucca spring blossoms:

- The ideal time to visit is in late March or early April to view the blooms in full bloom.
- Wear comfy shoes since you'll be walking a lot.
- Bring your camera to capture the splendor of the spring flowers.
- Try some of the area's springtime delicacies, such as fresh gelato and cantuccini pastries.

I wish you a lovely time visiting Lucca in the spring!

Summer's Festive Vibes

Summer is a period for festivals, concerts, and other special events in Lucca. Here are just a handful of the celebratory moods you can expect to see in Lucca this summer:

Lucca Summer Festival: Every summer, this world-renowned music festival takes place in Piazza Napoleone, Lucca's main plaza. The schedule includes worldwide and Italian acts ranging from rock and pop to jazz and classical. Bob Dylan, Elton John, Lenny Kravitz, and Paolo Nutini have all performed in the past. Lucca Summer Festival takes place in Lucca, Italy.

Lucca Jazz Festival: The Lucca Jazz Festival takes held in July at Piazza del Suffragio, a lovely area in the center of Lucca. The roster includes emerging jazz musicians from throughout the globe.

Lucca Film Festival: In July, the Cinema Centrale in Lucca hosts an international film festival.

The program includes both indie and popular films from Italy and throughout the globe.

Lucca Comics & Games: In October, Lucca hosts this major comics and gaming expo. The conference includes a massive exhibit hall with exhibitors from all over the globe, as well as seminars, discussions, and performances.

Lucca Film Festival: The Lucca Medieval Festival takes held in July at Lucca's Piazza Napoleone. The event recreates medieval life, complete with jousting competitions, falconry demonstrations, and traditional music and dance.

The Lucca Medieval Festival is held in Lucca, Italy.

In addition to these big festivals, there are a number of smaller events held in Lucca throughout the year. Food festivals, street festivals, and wine festivals are examples of such gatherings. There is always something to do in Lucca throughout the summer, so make your plans soon!

Here are some suggestions for enjoying Lucca's summer festivities:

- Purchase your tickets in early: Because many of Lucca's biggest festivals sell out rapidly, it is a good idea to purchase your tickets in advance.
- Dress comfortably: The summer weather in Lucca may be hot and humid, so bring comfortable clothes.
- Bring a hat and sunscreen: In the summer, the sun may be quite intense, so be sure to shield yourself from its rays.
- Pace yourself: Lucca has a lot to see and do, so don't attempt to do it all in one day. Take your time and enjoy yourself.

I hope this gives you a flavor of Lucca's summer festivities! If you are searching for a city that knows how to party, Lucca is the place to be.

Autumn's Golden Hues

The Piazza del Campo is one of the nicest sites in Lucca to experience fall. The Palazzo Pubblico and the Torre Guinigi are among the beautiful structures that surround this huge area. People go to the square in the autumn to enjoy the mild weather and changing foliage. The Botanical Garden is another fantastic site to view fall in Lucca. This garden is home to a diverse assortment of flora, and the leaves of the trees turn a magnificent crimson, orange, and yellow in the autumn. The garden is a wonderful location to unwind and appreciate nature's splendor.

Take a stroll or ride your bike around the city walls for a more active approach to enjoying fall in Lucca. The walls provide wonderful views of the surrounding landscape, and the leaves of the trees form a colorful canopy above in the autumn. Autumn is a lovely season in Lucca, no matter how you experience it. The city is full of beauty, and the mild weather makes it an ideal time to visit.

Here are some particular recommendations for fall activities in Lucca:

- Visit the Piazza del Campo to see the city's architecture.
- Take a stroll or ride your bike around the city walls to enjoy the autumn beauty.
- See the changing leaves in the Botanical Garden.
- Attend a concert or festival in one of the numerous squares or parks in Lucca.
- Try native food, which is made with fresh seasonal ingredients.
- Relax with a drink of wine or coffee at one of Lucca's numerous cafés or pubs.

Here are some other suggestions for organizing an autumn vacation to Lucca:

- From late September to early November is the greatest time to visit Lucca in the fall.

- Pack comfy shoes since you will be doing a lot of walking.
- Bring a jacket or sweater since the nights may be chilly.
- There is so much to see and do in the city that you should allow plenty of time to explore it.
- Try the local food, which is among the finest in Italy.
- Because Lucca is a popular tourist destination, be sure to reserve your lodgings in advance.

Winter's Cozy Charms

Take a stroll or ride your bike around the city walls. The walls stretch for about two kilometers and provide breathtaking views of the city and surrounding countryside. The walls are less busy in the winter than in the summer, making it an ideal time for a leisurely walk.

Pay a visit to the Piazza dell'Anfiteatro. This lovely area is situated in the city center and is flanked by historic structures. The area is turned into a Christmas market throughout the winter, with kiosks offering traditional cuisine, crafts, and presents.

Dine in a little bistro. Many great restaurants providing traditional Tuscan food may be found in Lucca. Many restaurants offer special winter menus throughout the winter, offering substantial meals like pasta e fagioli and ribollita.

Attend a culinary lesson. A local chef will teach you how to cook classic Tuscan cuisine. This is an excellent method to learn about Italian culture and food.

Go to a museum. The Museo Nazionale di Villa Guinigi, which has a collection of Renaissance art, and the Museo del Fumetto, which is devoted to comics and cartoons, are two of Lucca's finest museums.

Let's go shopping. Many businesses in Lucca offer typical Tuscan items such as leather goods, pottery, and olive oil. Many stores offer discounts and special promotions throughout the winter.

Go to a concert or the opera. Lucca has many music halls and opera houses that host a range of events throughout the year. Many locations host unique Christmas concerts and shows over the winter.

If you're searching for a warm and lovely winter getaway, Lucca is the place to be. Lucca will make your winter holiday memorable with its historic walls, attractive squares, and vibrant atmosphere.

Here are some more suggestions for organizing your winter visit to Lucca:

- The winter months to visit Lucca are December through February. The weather is pleasant at this time of year, and there are several celebratory activities going place.
- Pack thick clothing since temperatures may fall below freezing at night. You should also bring an umbrella or raincoat since it may rain or snow in the winter.
- If you want to visit any museums or churches, be sure to verify their hours of operation in advance. During the winter, many museums and cathedrals shut for the day in the afternoon.
- While in Lucca, be sure to sample some of the local food. Pasta e fagioli, ribollita, and

lampredotto (a sort of tripe sandwich) are among the most popular foods.

- Don't forget to stroll or ride your bike around the city walls. The city and surrounding area may be seen from the walls.

- In the winter, enjoy the festive atmosphere in Lucca. Throughout the city, there are several Christmas markets and other festive activities.

Lucca Travel Planner 🪐

Date: _____

Destination: _____

Address: _____   Transportation: _____

What To Do	Location
---	------------------------------
---	------------------------------
---	------------------------------
---	------------------------------
---	------------------------------
---	------------------------------
---	------------------------------
---	------------------------------

Note: _____

_____

_____

CHAPTER 6

Outdoor Activities

This enchanting city, beyond its quaint streets and medieval walls, provides a multitude of outdoor activities that enable tourists to discover its natural beauty and partake in adventurous experiences. Lucca's outdoor attractions are a testimony to its attractiveness, ranging from leisurely strolls atop the ancient walls to cycling across the scenic countryside.

Cycling the Lucca Walls

Cycling is an excellent method to discover the Lucca Walls. It's a reasonably straightforward journey that lets you see more of the city in less time. You may also snap images at any time along the trip. The Porta Elisa, one of the major gates in the walls, is the finest point to start your bicycle journey. Follow the signs for the ciclovia, which is the cycling route that runs along the top of the walls, from here.

The cycling route is large and well-maintained, making it a safe ride for cyclists of all skill levels. There are also several seats along the path where you may relax. You'll get amazing views of the city and surrounding countryside as you ride around the walls. You'll also see some of Lucca's most iconic sights, including the Duomo, the Guinigi Tower, and the Piazza dell'Anfiteatro. The bicycle trip lasts around an hour, but you may take as much time as you like. Along the journey, there are several spots to stop and explore.

Here's how to cycle the Lucca Walls:

- Begin your journey at Porta San Frediano. This is the main entrance to the city walls, and it is situated in Lucca's southeast corner.
- Circumambulate the walls clockwise. This is the most popular option since it provides the greatest views of the city.

- Come to a halt at the bastions. There are eleven bastions around the walls that provide excellent spots to rest and take in the landscape.
- Go to the gardens. Along the walls, there are various gardens, including the Giardino Botanico and the Giardino di S. Francesco.
- Your journey will come to an end in Porta Elisa. This is the major entrance to the city walls on Lucca's western side.

Here are some riding suggestions for the Lucca Walls:

- Put on some comfy sneakers. You'll be walking a lot, so make sure your shoes are comfortable.
- Bring a hat and sunscreen. Because the sun may be harsh in Tuscany, it is essential to protect oneself from the elements.
- Bring some water. Staying hydrated is critical, particularly in hot temperatures.

- Keep an eye on your surroundings. People often walk, run, and bike along the walls, so take care not to clash with anybody.
- Have fun on the ride! Cycling the Lucca Walls is a terrific opportunity to explore the city from a different perspective.

Here are some more things to consider while riding the Lucca Walls:

- From 7 a.m. until 11 p.m., the walls are open.
- In Lucca, renting a bike costs a minimal charge.
- You may also hire electric bikes, which are useful if you are unfamiliar with pedaling uphill.
- There are a number of bike rental businesses in Lucca, so you should have no problem locating one.
- Cycling the Lucca Walls is an excellent opportunity to get some exercise, visit the city, and take in the beauty. It's a must-do activity for every Lucca tourist.

Here are some more things to think about while organizing your riding trip:

- When the temperature is cooler, cycling the walls is best done in the morning or evening.
- There are various bike rental shops in Lucca.
- Along the trip, there are various spots to secure your bike.
- When riding, keep an eye out for pedestrians and other riders.
- Follow the driving laws.

Hiking in the Apuan Alps

The Apuan Alps are a mountain range in Tuscany, Italy, situated in the northwestern part of the country. They are a popular hiking destination, with a range of paths ranging from simple to difficult. The mountains are home to a multitude of breathtaking waterfalls, caves, and vistas, making them an ideal location for exploring Tuscany's natural splendor.

For guests, here is a trekking guide to the Apuan Alps:

How to Get There: The Apuan Alps are readily accessible from Lucca. There are many bus and rail routes that travel between Lucca and the mountain communities. Once in the mountains, there are a number of car parks at the beginning of popular routes.

When to go: The ideal seasons for trekking in the Apuan Alps are spring and autumn, when the weather is moderate and there are fewer tourists. The mountains are especially lovely in the winter when the snow-capped summits create a stunning background for your journey.

What to wear: It is recommended to dress in layers while trekking in the Apuan Alps so that you can react to changing weather conditions. Wear sturdy hiking boots or shoes with strong ankle support as well.

What to carry: In addition to the necessities like water, food, and sunscreen, you should bring a map, compass, and first aid kit. Warm clothes and snow gear are also required while trekking in the mountains during the winter.

Hiking paths: There are several hiking trails in the Apuan Alps, ranging from simple to difficult. Among the most popular trails are:

The Foce di Mosceta path: This is a difficult 10-kilometer track that leads you to the summit of the Foce di Mosceta Pass, where you can enjoy spectacular views of the surrounding mountains.

The Grotta del Vento walk: This simple 2-kilometer trail leads to the entrance of the Grotta del Vento cave, one of Italy's biggest caverns.

The Cascate del Dardagna trail: This easy 4-kilometer hike leads to a succession of waterfalls, including the Cascate del Dardagna, the highest waterfall in the Apuan Alps.

Hiking in the Apuan Alps may be a safe pastime provided the proper measures are taken. Make sure someone knows where you're going and when you intend to return. Also, keep an eye on the weather and dress properly. If you're going on a winter hike in the mountains, be sure to check the avalanche prediction first.

114

Water Sports along the Coast

Lucca is a lovely city in Tuscany, Italy, famous for its ancient walls and many churches and palaces. Lucca, on the other hand, has a lovely coastline with various beaches and chances for water sports.

Here is a list of some of the top water activities on the Lucca coast:

Sailing: Sailing is a terrific way to explore the coastline and take in the scenery. In Lucca, there are various sailing schools that provide instruction as well as boat rentals.

Windsurfing: Another excellent way to enjoy the wind and waves is to go windsurfing. In Lucca, there are various windsurfing schools that provide instruction and equipment rentals.

Kitesurfing: This is a more difficult water activity, but it is also a lot of fun. In Lucca, there are numerous kitesurfing schools that provide training and equipment rentals.

Stand-up paddleboarding: This is a terrific way to get some fitness while also enjoying the water. In Lucca, there are numerous stand-up paddleboarding schools that provide training and equipment rentals.

Canoeing: Canoeing is a terrific way to explore the shoreline while relaxing. In Lucca, there are various canoeing schools that provide instruction as well as canoe rentals.

Kayaking: Another fantastic option to explore the coastline and enjoy the peace and quiet is to go kayaking. In Lucca, there are various kayaking schools that provide instruction as well as kayak rentals.

Snorkeling: Snorkelling is an excellent method to explore the Mediterranean Sea's underwater ecosystem. There are various snorkeling locations along the Lucca coast.

Scuba diving: Scuba diving is a more sophisticated water activity, but it is an excellent opportunity to explore the Mediterranean Sea's underwater ecosystem. In Lucca, there are various scuba diving schools that provide training and equipment rentals.

Whatever your skill level or interests are, there is certain to be a water activity along the coast of Lucca that you will like. So get out there and discover!

Here are some further recommendations for water activities near the Lucca coast:

- Check the weather forecast before you leave: Make sure the weather is acceptable for the water activity you intend to participate in.
- Wear suitable clothes and footwear: Dress comfortably and without restricting your mobility. Wear footwear that protects your feet from pebbles and sand.
- Bring a hat and sunscreen: Take precautions against the sun's rays.
- Keep hydrated: Drink lots of water before, during, and after participating in water sports.
- Keep an eye on your surroundings: Keep an eye out for other persons and vessels in the water.

- Follow these safety precautions: Always adhere to the safety standards given out by the water sports school or instructor.

You may enjoy water activities along the coast of Lucca securely and have a fantastic time with a little forethought and preparation.

Lucca Travel Planner 🪐

Date: _____

Destination: _____

Address: _____   Transportation: _____

What To Do	Location
....	....
....	....
....	....
....	....
....	....
....	....
....	....
....	....

Note: _____
_____
_____

119

CHAPTER 7

Culinary Delights

L ucca provides a gourmet experience that will tickle the taste senses and leave a lasting impression on every tourist with a love for food.

Traditional Tuscan food is one of the hallmarks of Lucca's gastronomic scene. The city is well-known for using fresh, locally produced ingredients as the cornerstone of its delectable cuisine.

Must-Try Dishes and Restaurants

If you like cuisine and are planning a trip to Lucca, you are in for a treat. This article will walk you through the must-try meals and restaurants in Lucca, ensuring that your gastronomic adventure is nothing short of spectacular.

Buccellato at Taddeucci: Let's start with a local favorite, the Buccellato. Taddeucci, a traditional bakery in Lucca, is well-known for its delectable Buccellato. This sweet bread contains raisins, anise seeds, and sometimes chocolate. The mix of flavors and the delicate texture make it an ideal accompaniment to a cup of coffee.

Pappa al Pomodoro at Buca di Sant'Antonio: For a taste of classic Tuscan food, visit Buca di Sant'Antonio. This legendary restaurant offers a delectable tomato and bread soup called Pappa al Pomodoro. The soup is created with ripe tomatoes, garlic, basil, and stale bread, and it is robust and tasty.

Tortelli Lucchesi at Ristorante Giglio: Ristorante Giglio is a Michelin-starred restaurant that provides an extraordinary dining experience. Tortelli Lucchesi, a sort of packed pasta, is one of their signature meals. These enormous, square-shaped pasta packages are filled with beef, spinach, and Parmesan cheese combination and served with a hearty meat sauce. The flavor and texture combo is just amazing.

Farro: Farro is an ancient wheat grain that is popular in Lucca cuisine. Farro is a wonderful source of fiber and protein, and it has a nutty flavor that goes well with other ingredients. It can be prepared in a number of ways, but it's most often used in soups, salads, and meat dishes.

Bistecca alla Fiorentina at Osteria da Pasquale: If you like meat, the Bistecca alla Fiorentina at Osteria da Pasquale is a must-try. This typical Florentine steak is a thick-cut T-bone steak grilled to perfection over an open flame. The flesh is seasoned with salt, pepper, and olive oil to produce a juicy and tasty steak that will leave you wanting more.

Cacciucco at Trattoria da Leo: Seafood lovers should visit Trattoria da Leo to try the Cacciucco, a classic Tuscan fish stew. This savory meal is created with a thick tomato-based broth with a variety of fish and shellfish. The flavors are bold, and the stew is generally served with crusty bread to soak up the delectable sauce.

Gelato at Gelateria Veneta: A trip to Italy isn't complete until you indulge in gelato, and Gelateria Veneta is the place to go in Lucca. This gelateria has a broad variety of flavors that are all produced using high-quality ingredients. Gelateria Veneta provides something for everyone, whether you favor traditional flavors like pistachio and stracciatella or more daring ones like lavender and saffron.

Pizza at Pizzeria da Felice: For a relaxed and tasty dinner, visit Pizzeria da Felice. This neighborhood favorite is well-known for its genuine Neapolitan-style pizza. The thin, crunchy dough, topped with fresh toppings and melting cheese, will whisk you away to pizza nirvana. Don't miss out on their trademark Margherita pizza, which exemplifies the simplicity and excellence of Italian food.

Panzanella at Osteria San Giorgio: Osteria San Giorgio is a charming restaurant that offers classic Tuscan meals with a contemporary touch. A must-try is their Panzanella, a bread and tomato salad. This delicious salad, made with stale bread, juicy tomatoes, cucumbers, onions, and basil, is ideal for a hot summer day.

Risotto al Tartufo at Ristorante Giglio: A truffle risotto is another great dish at Ristorante Giglio. Carnaroli rice, Parmesan cheese, and black truffles combine to make this creamy and flavorful meal. The earthy truffle flavors paired with the creaminess of the risotto produce a wonderfully decadent experience.

Cantucci with Vin Santo at Pasticceria Taddeucci: To complete your gastronomic adventure on a sweet note, return to Taddeucci and enjoy their Cantucci with Vin Santo. Cantucci is almond cookies commonly dunked in Vin Santo, a sweet dessert wine. The crisp cookie paired with the sweet wine is a marriage made in heaven.

124

Here are some of the top Lucca places to taste these dishes:

Buca di Sant'Antonio: A local favorite, this tiny trattoria. Tordelli Lucchesi, farro soup, and baccalà alla Lucchese are among the classic Tuscan foods served.

Trattoria da Giulio: This family-run restaurant serves classic Tuscan cuisine. They also provide a broad assortment of regional wines.

La Bottega di Anna e Leo: This lovely osteria offers delectable home-cooked dishes. They provide pasta, including tordelli Lucchesi, as well as beef and seafood dishes.

Osteria del Sole: Located in the center of Lucca, this ancient eatery. They provide traditional Tuscan cooking as well as some more inventive stuff.

Enoteca Cipriani: This wine bar is an excellent spot to sample some of the region's wines. They also provide a limited selection of pasta meals and snacks.

Local Markets

Lucca has multiple marketplaces, each with its own distinct personality. *Here's a quick rundown of some of the most popular markets:*

The Forno Boario Farmers Market: This is open every Saturday and Wednesday morning from 8 a.m. to 1 p.m. at the Foro Boario, a nineteenth-century market hall near the San Quirico Bridge. The market is an excellent source of fresh, locally produced fruits, vegetables, meats, cheeses, and other culinary items. There are also a few vendors offering handcrafted items and souvenirs.

The Piazza San Francesco Farmers Market: This is held every Wednesday afternoon from 4 p.m. to 7:30 p.m. at Piazza San Francesco, a lovely plaza in the center of Lucca. Although the market is smaller than the Forno Boario Farmers Market, it nonetheless provides a large range of fresh, local products. There are also some vendors offering handcrafted items and souvenirs.

The Il Mercatino Flea Market: Held every Sunday morning from 8 a.m. to 1 p.m. at Via per Chiatri, a street just outside the city walls. Antiques, collectibles, vintage clothes, and other secondhand products may be found at the market. There are also other food kiosks providing snacks and beverages.

The Christmas Market: From late November through December, this market is hosted at Piazza Napoleone. A variety of vendors offer Christmas decorations, ornaments, presents, and food during the market. A Ferris wheel and a variety of other rides and attractions are also available.

In addition to these regular markets, a variety of special markets are hosted throughout the year. These markets may specialize in a particular product, such as olive oil or wine, or they may be themed around a certain festival or event.

Whatever your hobbies are, you'll find something to your liking at one of Lucca's local markets. So, while planning your vacation to this lovely city, be sure to include a market visit.

Here are some recommendations for visiting Lucca's local markets:

- Arrive early, particularly if coming on a weekend or during the summer. The markets may get congested, and the finest booths sometimes sell out quickly.
- Put on some comfy sneakers. You'll be on your feet a lot!
- Bring a reusable bag with you to carry your purchases in.
- Be prepared to bargain. This is particularly prevalent in flea markets.
- Take in the atmosphere! Local markets are an excellent opportunity to learn about Italian culture and enjoy some of the region's delectable cuisine.

128

Lucca Event Calendar 2024

- Lucca Comics & Games (October 27-30, 2024): One of Europe's biggest and most popular comic book conventions, this four-day event is held in Lucca, Italy. It draws over 200,000 people each year and offers a variety of events including seminars, discussions, readings, and performances.

- Lucca Summer event (June 20-August 27, 2024): This music event takes place at Piazza Napoleone and showcases an international and Italian roster of musicians. Sting, Elton John, and David Bowie have all performed in the past.

- Lucca Marathon (April 22, 2024): This race brings runners through Lucca's medieval city walls. A half marathon and a 10K event are also available.

- Lucca Jazz Festival (July 1-22, 2024): This jazz festival is held in several locations across the city.

Chick Corea, Herbie Hancock, and Miles Davis have all performed in the past.

- The Lucca Opera Festival (July 15-August 26, 2024) takes place in the courtyard of the Palazzo Ducale. Plácido Domingo, Luciano Pavarotti, and Maria Callas have all performed in the past.

- Lucca Film Festival (April 25–May 6, 2024): This festival features independent and international films. Previous films include "The Godfather," "Casablanca," and "Lagaan."

- The Lucca Medieval Festival (June 23-25, 2024) commemorates Lucca's medieval past with jousting competitions, sword battles, and historical reenactments.

- Lucca Christmas Market (November 24-December 24, 2024): Located in Piazza Napoleone, this Christmas market has vendors offering Christmas decorations, food, and drink. A Ferris wheel and a carousel are also available.

These are just a handful of the many events held in Lucca throughout the year. Please visit the official tourist website of Lucca for additional information.

Here are some more suggestions for organizing a vacation to Lucca in 2024:

- Book your lodgings in advance: Because Lucca is a popular tourist destination, it is necessary to book your accommodations in advance, particularly if you are visiting during peak season.
- Get a city pass: There are many city cards available in Lucca that may save you money on museums, attractions, and tour entrances.
- Take advantage of free activities: Throughout the year, Lucca hosts a variety of free events including concerts, festivals, and markets.
- While English is frequently spoken in Lucca, it is always beneficial to acquire a few basic Italian phrases.

- Enjoy the local cuisine: Lucca has numerous outstanding restaurants that serve authentic Tuscan cuisine.
- Explore the surrounding countryside and towns: Because Lucca is situated in the heart of Tuscany, there are several possibilities to explore the surrounding countryside and towns.

Lucca Travel Planner 🪐

Date: _____

Destination: _____

Address: _____ Transportation: _____

What To Do	Location
....	....
....	....
....	....
....	....
....	....
....	....
....	....
....	....
....	....
....	....

Note: ....
....
....

CHAPTER 8

Day Trips from Lucca

L ucca, in Tuscany, Italy, is a picturesque city famed for its well-preserved Renaissance walls, cobblestone streets, and exquisite architecture. It's an excellent starting point for exploring the surrounding area. *Here are some great day trip ideas from Lucca:*

Florence

Florence is one of Italy's most famous tourist destinations for good reason. Some of the world's most renowned pieces of art, architecture, and history may be found in the city. But what if you just have a day and can only visit for a day? Don't worry, there's enough to see and do in Florence in a single day. Here is a schedule for a memorable day excursion from Lucca:

In the morning, Begin your day by visiting the Uffizi Gallery. This internationally renowned museum has a significant collection of Renaissance art, including pieces by Botticelli, Michelangelo, and Leonardo da Vinci. After seeing the Uffizi, wander around Piazza della Signoria. The Palazzo Vecchio, the municipal hall, and the Fountain of Neptune are all located in this magnificent area.

In the afternoon, Enjoy a classic Tuscan meal at one of the numerous eateries in the neighborhood for lunch. Climb to the top of the Duomo in the afternoon. This imposing church has commanding views of the city.

In the Evening, Take a leisurely walk around the Boboli Gardens in the evening. These lovely gardens are situated behind the Pitti Palace and are a wonderful spot to unwind and enjoy an Italian evening. Try one of Florence's numerous Michelin-starred restaurants for supper. After dinner, go to one of the city's numerous bustling pubs or clubs for a drink.

Of course, this is just a suggestion, and you may tailor the schedule to your own interests and time limits. However, no matter how you spend your day in Florence, you will have a fantastic experience.

Here are some more suggestions for organizing a day trip to Florence from Lucca:

- Plan ahead of time for your train tickets, particularly if you're traveling during high season.
- Purchase advance skip-the-line tickets for the Uffizi Gallery and the Duomo. This will save you a significant amount of time waiting in line.
- Wear comfy shoes since you'll be walking a lot.
- Bring a camera to record your memories.
- Prepare to be awestruck by Florence's beauty and history.

Pisa

Pisa is a lovely Tuscany city well known for its famous Leaning Tower. But Pisa is more than simply its famous tower. Pisa is a fascinating day excursion from Lucca, with its rich history, gorgeous architecture, and wonderful cuisine.

A proposed schedule for a day excursion to Pisa from Lucca is as follows:

Morning: Begin your day in Lucca by visiting Piazza dell'Anfiteatro. This lovely plaza was formerly the location of a Roman amphitheater and is now popular with both residents and visitors. From there, stroll to the Duomo di Lucca, a spectacular Gothic-style cathedral.

Afternoon: Travel from Lucca to Pisa by rail or bus. When you arrive in Pisa, go to the Piazza dei Miracoli, which houses the Leaning Tower of Pisa, the Duomo di Pisa, and the Baptistery of Pisa. Spend some time visiting these wonderful sights, and don't forget to photograph the Leaning Tower from the correct perspective!

Evening: Before taking your train or bus back to Lucca, stop in Pisa for a great meal.

Here are some more ideas for organizing a day trip to Pisa from Lucca:

- Pisa is best visited in the spring or autumn when the weather is moderate and there are fewer people.

- If you want to see the Leaning Tower of Pisa, be sure you get your tickets in advance. Tickets may easily sell out, particularly during high season.

- There are various options for getting from Lucca to Pisa. You may go by rail, bus, or cab. The train is the quickest alternative, taking around 30 minutes to travel between the two cities.

- There are various free things to do in Pisa if you're on a tight budget. You may tour the Boboli Gardens, the Piazza dei Miracoli, and the city walls.

Cinque Terre

Cinque Terre is a collection of five settlements perched on the cliffs of the Italian Riviera. It is a UNESCO World Heritage Site as well as one of Italy's most popular tourist sites. Riomaggiore, Manarola, Corniglia, Vernazza, and Monterosso al Mare are the settlements. A day excursion from Lucca to Cinque Terre is an excellent opportunity to see this stunning region of Italy. Lucca is a lovely city with an intact medieval center. It is around an hour's drive from Cinque Terre.

There are many options for getting from Lucca to Cinque Terre. You have the option of taking the train, bus, or vehicle. The railway is the most picturesque mode of transportation since it follows the coastline and provides breathtaking views of the towns. The bus is a more cost-effective choice, although it is slower and less picturesque. The automobile is the most convenient mode of transportation, however, parking in Cinque Terre may be tough to come by.

You may tour the towns on foot after you get to Cinque Terre. There are hiking paths connecting the settlements, as well as lots of places to eat and drink.

A proposed route for day travel from Lucca to Cinque Terre is as follows:

Early in the morning, take the train from Lucca to Riomaggiore. This is Cinque Terre's first settlement. Spend some time wandering the winding alleys and brightly colored residences. Lunch will be served in Riomaggiore.

Take the train from Riomaggiore to Manarola in the afternoon. This is Cinque Terre's second settlement. Manarola is well-known for its breathtaking views of the surrounding vineyards and sea. Spend some time wandering around the cliffs and taking in the scenery. Dinner will be served in Manarola.

Later in the evening, take the train from Manarola to Vernazza. This is Cinque Terre's third settlement. Vernazza is notable for its harbor and castle. Spend some time touring the town and taking in the coastal views. Return to Lucca via rail.

This is simply a recommended schedule; you may tailor it to your own interests and time limitations. There is no correct or incorrect way to enjoy Cinque Terre.

Here are some pointers to help you organize your day excursion from Lucca to Cinque Terre:

- Purchase your rail tickets in advance, particularly if traveling during high season.
- Wear comfy shoes since you will be walking a lot.
- Because the weather in Cinque Terre may be hot and sunny, bring sunscreen and a hat.
- Bring a camera since you'll want to capture all of the breathtaking scenery.

- Expect crowds, particularly during the warmer months.
- Have a wonderful day! Cinque Terre is an enchanted spot.

Siena

Siena, in Tuscany, Italy, is a charming city that is well worth a day trip from Lucca. The two cities are just approximately an hour apart by vehicle, making it simple to travel between them. Siena's historic center is a tangle of small alleys, ancient houses, and large piazzas, and it is a UNESCO World Heritage Site. The most well-known of these piazzas is Piazza del Campo, which hosts the Palio di Siena, a centuries-old horse race held twice a year.

The Duomo, the Piccolomini Library, and the Santa Maria della Scala Museum complex are among the must-sees in Siena. The Duomo is a Gothic cathedral with a beautiful interior, and the Piccolomini Library has an illuminated manuscript collection.

The museum complex of Santa Maria della Scala is a former hospital that now contains a range of art and artifacts. Siena is well-known for its exquisite cuisine, in addition to its rich history and culture. Try some local favorites like pici, a sort of thick spaghetti, and panforte, a typical Tuscan confection.

A proposed schedule for a day excursion to Siena from Lucca is as follows:

Morning: Begin your day by seeing the Duomo. Climb to the top of the bell tower for panoramic views of the city.

Afternoon: Walk around Piazza del Campo and observe the surrounding architecture. You may even catch the Palio di Siena if you're fortunate.

Evening: Dine at a local restaurant for a typical Tuscan supper. Try some of the regional delicacies, such as pici and panforte.

If you have more time, you may also pay a visit to the Piccolomini Library or the Santa Maria della Scala Museum complex in Siena.

Here are some other suggestions for organizing your Siena day trip:

- The finest seasons to visit Siena are spring and autumn when the weather is warm.
- If you want to come during the Palio di Siena, be sure to get your tickets in advance.
- There are many methods to go from Lucca to Siena. You have the option of taking the train, bus, or vehicle.
- It's simple to navigate about Siena on foot after you've arrived.
- When shopping for souvenirs, remember to haggle.

San Gimignano

San Gimignano is a lovely medieval town in the Italian region of Tuscany. It is roughly an hour's drive from Lucca and makes an excellent day excursion from there. San Gimignano is well-known for its 14 medieval towers that soar over the town's skyline. The towers were erected in the 13th and 14th centuries by affluent families as a reminder of the town's golden history.

San Gimignano, in addition to its towers, features a variety of additional attractions, including:

- The major plaza of the town, Piazza del Duomo.
- The San Gimignano Collegiate Church is a stunning Gothic church.
- The National Pinacoteca of San Gimignano, includes a collection of paintings dating from the 13th to the 16th century.
- The Civic Museum, which displays local archaeological findings.

145

- San Gimignano also has a variety of stores and restaurants where you may try local cuisine and wine.

- You may take a bus or rail from Lucca to San Gimignano. The bus is the most affordable choice, although it takes a bit longer. The train is more costly, but it is also speedier.

- You may explore San Gimignano on foot after you arrive. The streets are tiny and twisting, making it easy to get disoriented. But that's half the joy!

- If you don't have much time, you may take a guided tour of the town. There are a variety of trips offered, so you may choose one that suits your interests.

Whatever you choose to do in San Gimignano, you will have an unforgettable experience. The town is lovely and old, and it's a terrific way to see the finest of Tuscany.

A proposed schedule for a day excursion to San Gimignano from Lucca is as follows:

- 9:00 a.m.: Take the train from Lucca to San Gimignano (about 1 hour).
- 10:00 a.m.: Arrive in San Gimignano and begin exploring.
- 12:00 PM: Eat lunch at a nearby restaurant.
- 1:00 PM: Visit the San Gimignano Collegiate Church.
- 2:00 PM: Go on a guided tour of the town.
- Visit the Civic Museum at 3:00 PM.
- 4:00 PM: Visit a local vineyard for some wine sampling.
- 5:00 PM: Return to Lucca by rail (approximately 1 hour).

This itinerary provides an excellent overview of the town and its attractions. You may tailor it to your own interests and time restrictions.

Here are some pointers to consider while organizing a day trip to San Gimignano:

- Plan ahead of time for your train tickets, particularly if you're traveling during the high season.
- Wear comfy shoes since you will be walking a lot.
- Because the weather might be scorching in the summer, bring sunscreen and a hat.
- Bring your camera since you'll want to capture all of San Gimignano's splendor.

Lucca Travel Planner

Date: _____

Destination: _____

Address: _____   Transportation: _____

What To Do   Location

_____   _____
_____   _____
_____   _____
_____   _____
_____   _____
_____   _____
_____   _____
_____   _____

Note: _____
_____
_____

CHAPTER 9

Language and Etiquette

L ucca's official language is Italian. However, many individuals in Lucca speak English, particularly those in the tourist business. Don't worry if you don't speak Italian. English will still allow you to get by in Lucca.

Here are some simple Italian phrases you may find useful:

- Hello: Ciao
- Goodbye: Arrivederci
- Please: Per favore
- Thank you: Grazie
- You're welcome: Prego
- Do you speak English?: Parla inglese?
- I don't speak Italian: Non parlo Italiano

Etiquette

In general, Italians are highly pleasant and inviting to guests. When it comes to etiquette in Lucca, there are a few things to bear in mind.

- Be aware of your body language. Italians stand closer to one another than individuals from other cultures. They also make extensive use of hand gestures. It might be overpowering if you're not accustomed to it.
- Don't be scared to strike up a conversation. Italians like a good discussion, so don't be hesitant to start up a conversation with your waiter, tour guide, or even a random stranger on the street.
- Put on proper clothing. Because Lucca is a conservative city, it is recommended to dress modestly. Shorts, tank tops, and flip-flops are not permitted.
- Be mindful of local traditions. When entering a church or other religious structure, dress properly

and take off your hat. Also, keep the noise level in mind. In public, Italians prefer to talk gently.

You may make your visit to Lucca more enjoyable by following these suggestions.

Here are a few more politeness recommendations for Lucca:

- It is normal to greet the personnel while entering a store or restaurant.
- When paying for a purchase, it is customary to round up to the closest euro.
- When tipping, a minimal amount is enough. A euro or two is generally plenty.
- Blowing your nose in public is considered impolite.
- It is customary to offer a little gift, like flowers or wine, when invited to someone's house for supper.

By following these suggestions, you may demonstrate to the people of Lucca that you value their culture and traditions.

Navigating Italian Customs with Ease

- Collect your paperwork. You'll need your passport, visa (if necessary), and any other papers needed to enter Italy. You should also have a copy of your airline itinerary and hotel information with you.
- Select the proper customs lane. When you go to customs, you'll see two lanes: green and red. The green lane is for those who have no items to report, whereas the red lane is for those who do. If you are unclear whether you need to disclose anything, always use the red lane.
- Show the customs officer your documentation. Present your papers to the customs officer when you reach the front of the queue. The officer will

inquire about your journey and may want to examine your bags.

- Declare any products you want to bring into Italy. If you bring into Italy any products that are subject to duty or taxes, you must disclose them to the customs officer. This includes alcoholic beverages, cigarettes, and technological devices.

- You must pay any relevant tariffs or taxes. If you have any tariffs or taxes to pay on your items, you will do so at the customs counter. You may pay with cash or with a credit card.

- Clear customs. You are allowed to depart the airport after you have completed customs.

Here are some more pointers for smoothly negotiating Italian customs:

- Prepare yourself. Before you arrive at customs, gather your paperwork and know what you're carrying into Italy.

- Be kind and cooperative. Customs agents are only performing their jobs, so be kind and answer their inquiries truthfully.
- Please be patient. Customs lines might be lengthy, so be patient and avoid becoming irritated.
- If you are prepared and know what to anticipate, navigating Italian customs may be a breeze. By following these suggestions, you may ensure a pleasant and trouble-free arrival in Italy.

Here are some more things to remember while navigating Italian traditions in Lucca:

- The Lucca airport terminal's customs office is on the ground level.
- The customs office is open from 6:00 a.m. to 10:00 p.m.
- If you arrive in Lucca from a country other than the EU, you may be subject to a random customs examination.

- If you have any questions concerning customs, it is usually better to seek a customs officer for help.

Cultural Dos and Don'ts

Dos:

- Dress appropriately. When visiting churches and other religious places, cover your shoulders and knees. It also implies that you should dress modestly in general. It is a good idea to follow the example of the Italians when it comes to fashion.

- Learn a few fundamental Italian phrases. This will demonstrate to the locals that you are making an attempt to understand and respect their culture. "Buongiorno" (Good morning) "Buonasera" (Good evening) "Grazie" (Thank you) "Prego" (You're welcome) "Scusi" (Excuse me) are some important words.

- Please be patient. Expect everything to take their time in Italy because they like to take their time. This is particularly true in the case of bureaucracy.
- Have fun with the food! Lucca has some of Italy's greatest cuisine. Try the tortelli lucchesi, a traditional local pasta dish.
- On foot, explore the city. Walking through Lucca's small alleyways and admiring the architecture is the best way to experience it.
- Relax on the Piazza dell'Anfiteatro. This lovely area in the heart of the city is the ideal location to unwind and people-watch.

Don'ts:

- Don't be too loud. Because Italians are typically quiet people, it is necessary to respect their noise levels. This includes speaking quietly in public and not playing music loudly.
- Don't be impolite to service employees. Because Italians appreciate civility and respect, it is

important to be kind to everyone you meet, particularly service personnel.

- Please do not litter. Because Italians take pleasure in their cleanliness, it is important that you dispose of your rubbish appropriately.
- Take no photographs of individuals without their consent. In Italy, this is considered impolite.
- Shorts and tank tops are not permitted in churches. This is considered impolite.

You may have a good and courteous time in Lucca if you follow these dos and don'ts.

Health Facilities and Emergency Contacts

As a tourist to Lucca, you should be informed of the accessible health facilities and emergency contacts.

Health Care Facilities

Visitors visiting Lucca may get medical attention at a number of hospitals and clinics. The Ospedale San Luca, situated on Via Guglielmo Lippi Francesconi, is the primary hospital. The emergency department of the Ospedale San Luca is available 24 hours a day. In Lucca, there are also some smaller clinics that may give basic medical treatment.

Emergency Phone Numbers

There are various numbers you may contact for assistance in an emergency. In Italy, the national emergency number is **112.** This number may be used to contact any form of emergency services, such as the police, fire department, or ambulance. You may also contact one of the numerous local emergency lines. The Ospedale San Luca's emergency number is **0583 055601.** The Lucca Fire Department's emergency number is **0583 430000.** The Lucca Police Department's emergency number is **0583 4551.**

Other Valuable Numbers

In addition to the emergency lines, there are numerous more numbers that you as a tourist to Lucca may find helpful. These figures are as follows:

- Tourist Information: +39 0583 4171
- Taxi: +39 025 353
- Bus: +39 0583 587 897
- Pharmacy: +39 0583 491 398

Keeping Fit in Lucca

There are certain things you can do to be healthy when visiting Lucca. First and foremost, drink lots of water, particularly if the weather is hot. Second, consume an abundance of fruits and vegetables. Third, avoid swimming in bodies of water with which you are unfamiliar. Finally, be sure you get enough rest.

Useful Phrases for Interaction

If you're going to Lucca, here are some words to help you communicate with locals and make the most of your stay there:

Greetings:

- "Ciao!" (informal)

- "Buongiorno!" (good morning)
- "Buonasera!" (good evening)

Polite phrases:

- "Per favore." (please)
- "Grazie." (thank you)
- "Prego." (you're welcome)
- "Mi scusi." (excuse me)

Directions:

- "Dove posso trovare...? (where can I find...?)
- "Come si arriva a...? (how do I get to...?)
- "Quanto dista...? (how far is it to...?)

Food and drink:

- "Cosa mi consiglia?" (what do you recommend?)
- "Un bicchiere d'acqua, per favore." (a glass of water, please)
- "Una birra, per favore." (a beer, please)

- "Una pizza, per favore." (a pizza, please)

Shopping:

- "Quanto costa...? (how much is...?)
- "Posso provare questo?" (can I try this on?)
- "Vorrei pagare, per favore." (I would like to pay, please)
- Other:
- "Non capisco." (I don't understand.)
- "Parli inglese?" (do you speak English?)
- "Mi piace molto Lucca." (I really like Lucca.)

These are just a handful of the most important terms to know while interacting in Lucca. You may express your admiration for the local culture and make your vacation even more pleasurable by learning a few words in Italian.

Here are some more recommendations for engaging with residents in Lucca:

- Be kind and respectful.
- When communicating with someone, make eye contact.
- When addressing somebody you don't know well, use formal language.
- If you want assistance, do not be hesitant to ask for it.
- Be patient, since not everyone will be proficient in English.

You may guarantee that your contacts with residents in Lucca are good and pleasurable by following these tips.

Local Etiquette and Culture

- We are sensitive to the old city center. Because Lucca's old center is a UNESCO World Heritage Site, visitors must respect the buildings and artifacts. Walking on the lawn, touching the walls, or taking pictures without permission are all prohibited.

- Wear something modest. Because Lucca is a conservative city, visitors should dress modestly. This includes covering your shoulders and knees and wearing modest apparel.

- Take note of your noise level. Because Lucca is a peaceful city, you should be aware of your noise level. Avoid generating loud noises or chatting loudly in public areas.

- Please be patient. Italians are renowned for their slow pace of life, thus patience is required while visiting Lucca. Expect things to take time, and don't get irritated if they don't go your way.

- Learn a few fundamental Italian phrases. Even if you don't speak Italian well, tourists who make an effort to acquire a few fundamental words are always welcome. This demonstrates that you are making an effort to understand and appreciate the culture.

- Give a large tip. Tipping is customary in Italy, so pay generously when you get excellent service. A typical gratuity is 10% of the cost.

- Be mindful of local traditions. When visiting Lucca, you should be aware of a few local traditions. For example, it is considered impolite to eat while walking, and it is not normal to greet someone with a kiss on the cheek.
- By following these suggestions, you may demonstrate your appreciation for Lucca's culture while also making the most of your stay.

Here are some further recommendations for Lucca visitors:

- Discover the history of Lucca. Lucca has a lengthy and illustrious history that dates back to the Etruscans. Learning about the city's past can help you understand its distinct culture.
- Visit the art museums and galleries. The Museo Nazionale di Villa Guinigi, the Pinacoteca Nazionale, and the Museo del Fumetto are just a few of Lucca's renowned museums and art galleries.

165

- Take a stroll around the historic district. A stroll around Lucca's old center is the greatest way to feel its allure. Visit the small alleyways, enjoy the architecture, and stop for a coffee or gelato at one of the numerous cafés.
- Enjoy the local cuisine. Lucca has numerous wonderful restaurants that serve traditional Tuscan food. Try local dishes like pasta al ragù, cacciucco (a seafood stew), and torta co' bischeri (a regional cake).
- Participate in a cultural event. Throughout the year, Lucca holds a variety of cultural events including concerts, festivals, and theatre performances. Check the events calendar to discover what's going on during your stay.

I hope these recommendations help you make the most of your trip to Lucca!

Conclusion

As the last part of the Lucca travel guide concludes, we say goodbye to this wonderful city with both nostalgia and anticipation. Lucca, with its rich history, lively culture, and stunning scenery, has definitely left an unforgettable imprint on the hearts of everyone who have had the opportunity to explore its treasures. In this last segment, we consider the many experiences available in Lucca. Lucca certainly captivates the senses, from wandering through the historic city walls that have withstood the test of time to immersing oneself in the melodic notes of the famed Puccini Festival.

The book emphasizes the city's architectural wonders, such as the beautiful Duomo di San Martino and the towering Guinigi Tower, giving readers an insight into the city's rich history. Furthermore, the book stresses the culinary joys that await travelers, such as savoring excellent Tuscan food at quaint trattorias and indulging in the city's famed gelato. It also urges readers to leave the city boundaries and explore the magnificent Tuscan

167

countryside, which is filled with vineyards and olive groves, as well as find hidden jewels such as the adjacent ancient village of Barga. As we come to the end of this travel guide, we encourage readers to go on their own Lucca trip, equipped with the information and insights given inside these pages. Lucca guarantees to create an indelible impression, whether it's a leisurely bike ride along the Serchio River or an evening promenade around the picturesque Piazza dell'Anfiteatro.

May this guide serve as a friend, leading visitors through the city's winding streets and revealing its mysteries. Farewell, my readers, and may your exploration of Lucca be filled with amazing memories and limitless discoveries.

Lucca Travel Planner

Date: _____

Destination: _____

Address: _____   Transportation: _____

What To Do	Location
------------------------------	------------------------------
------------------------------	------------------------------
------------------------------	------------------------------
------------------------------	------------------------------
------------------------------	------------------------------
------------------------------	------------------------------
------------------------------	------------------------------
------------------------------	------------------------------
------------------------------	------------------------------

Note: _____
_____
_____

Lucca Travel Planner

Date: _____

Destination: _____

Address: _____ Transportation: _____

What To Do	Location
-------------------------	-------------------------
-------------------------	-------------------------
-------------------------	-------------------------
-------------------------	-------------------------
-------------------------	-------------------------
-------------------------	-------------------------
-------------------------	-------------------------
-------------------------	-------------------------

Note: _____

_____

_____

Lucca Travel Planner

Date: _____

Destination: _____

Address: _____   Transportation: _____

What To Do	Location
----------------------------------	----------------------------------
----------------------------------	----------------------------------
----------------------------------	----------------------------------
----------------------------------	----------------------------------
----------------------------------	----------------------------------
----------------------------------	----------------------------------
----------------------------------	----------------------------------
----------------------------------	----------------------------------
----------------------------------	----------------------------------

Note: _____
_____
_____

Lucca Travel Planner

Date: _____

Destination: _____

Address: _____   **Transportation:** _____

What To Do	Location

Note: _____
_____
_____

Lucca Travel Planner 🪐

Date: _____

Destination: _____

Address: _____ Transportation: _____

What To Do	Location
....	....
....	....
....	....
....	....
....	....
....	....
....	....
....	....

Note: ....
....
....

Lucca Travel Planner 🪐

Date: _____

Destination: _ _ _ _ _ _ _ _ _ _ _ _ _ _ _

Address: _____   Transportation: _____

What To Do	Location
------------------------------	------------------------------
------------------------------	------------------------------
------------------------------	------------------------------
------------------------------	------------------------------
------------------------------	------------------------------
------------------------------	------------------------------
------------------------------	------------------------------
------------------------------	------------------------------
------------------------------	------------------------------

Note: _____

_____

_____

Lucca Travel Planner

Date: _____

Destination: _____

Address: _____ Transportation: _____

What To Do	Location

Note: _____

Lucca Travel Planner

Date: _____

Destination: _____

Address: _____ Transportation: _____

What To Do	Location

Note: _____
_____
_____

Lucca Travel Planner

Date: _____

Destination: _____

Address: _____ Transportation: _____

What To Do	Location
---------------------------	---------------------------
---------------------------	---------------------------
---------------------------	---------------------------
---------------------------	---------------------------
---------------------------	---------------------------
---------------------------	---------------------------
---------------------------	---------------------------
---------------------------	---------------------------
---------------------------	---------------------------

Note: _____

_____

_____

Lucca Travel Planner

Date: _____

Destination: _____

Address: _____   Transportation: _____

What To Do	Location

Note: _____
_____
_____

Lucca Travel Planner

Date: _____

Destination: _____

Address: _____   Transportation: _____

What To Do	Location
----------------------------------	-------------------
----------------------------------	-------------------
----------------------------------	-------------------
----------------------------------	-------------------
----------------------------------	-------------------
----------------------------------	-------------------
----------------------------------	-------------------
----------------------------------	-------------------

Note: _____
_____
_____

Lucca Travel Planner

Date: _____

Destination: _____

Address: _____   Transportation: _____

What To Do	Location
----------------------------------	----------------------------------
----------------------------------	----------------------------------
----------------------------------	----------------------------------
----------------------------------	----------------------------------
----------------------------------	----------------------------------
----------------------------------	----------------------------------
----------------------------------	----------------------------------
----------------------------------	----------------------------------
----------------------------------	----------------------------------

Note: _____
_____
_____

Lucca Travel Planner

Date: _____

Destination: _____

Address: _____   Transportation: _____

What To Do	Location
....	....
....	....
....	....
....	....
....	....
....	....
....	....
....	....
....	....

Note: ....

....

....

Lucca Travel Planner

Date: _____

Destination: _____

Address: _____ Transportation: _____

What To Do

Location

------------------------------------ ------------------------------------

------------------------------------ ------------------------------------

------------------------------------ ------------------------------------

------------------------------------ ------------------------------------

------------------------------------ ------------------------------------

------------------------------------ ------------------------------------

------------------------------------ ------------------------------------

------------------------------------ ------------------------------------

Note: _____

_____

_____

Lucca Travel Planner 🪐

Date: _____

Destination: _____

Address: _____   Transportation: _____

What To Do	Location
....	....
....	....
....	....
....	....
....	....
....	....
....	....
....	....
....	....

Note: ....
....
....

Lucca Travel Planner

Date: _____

Destination: _____

Address: _____   Transportation: _____

What To Do	Location
_____	_____
_____	_____
_____	_____
_____	_____
_____	_____
_____	_____
_____	_____
_____	_____
_____	_____

Note: _____

_____

_____

Lucca Travel Planner

Date: _____

Destination: _____

Address: _____ Transportation: _____

What To Do	Location
....	....
....	....
....	....
....	....
....	....
....	....
....	....
....	....

Note: ....

....

....

Lucca Travel Planner

Date: _____

Destination: _____

Address: _____   Transportation: _____

What To Do   Location

------------------------------   ------------------------------
------------------------------   ------------------------------
------------------------------   ------------------------------
------------------------------   ------------------------------
------------------------------   ------------------------------
------------------------------   ------------------------------
------------------------------   ------------------------------
------------------------------   ------------------------------
------------------------------   ------------------------------

Note: _____
_____
_____

Lucca Travel Planner

Date: _____

Destination: _____

Address: _____ Transportation: _____

What To Do	Location
----------------------------------	----------------------------------
----------------------------------	----------------------------------
----------------------------------	----------------------------------
----------------------------------	----------------------------------
----------------------------------	----------------------------------
----------------------------------	----------------------------------
----------------------------------	----------------------------------
----------------------------------	----------------------------------
----------------------------------	----------------------------------

Note: _____

_____

_____

Lucca Travel Planner

Date: _____

Destination: _____

Address: _____ Transportation: _____

What To Do	Location
----------------------------------	----------------------------------
----------------------------------	----------------------------------
----------------------------------	----------------------------------
----------------------------------	----------------------------------
----------------------------------	----------------------------------
----------------------------------	----------------------------------
----------------------------------	----------------------------------
----------------------------------	----------------------------------

Note: _____

_____

_____

Lucca Travel Planner

Date: _____

Destination: _____

Address: _____   **Transportation:** _____

What To Do	Location
....	....
....	....
....	....
....	....
....	....
....	....
....	....
....	....

Note: ....
....
....

189

Lucca Travel Planner

Date: _____

Destination: _____

Address: _____   Transportation: _____

What To Do	Location
----------------------------	----------------------------
----------------------------	----------------------------
----------------------------	----------------------------
----------------------------	----------------------------
----------------------------	----------------------------
----------------------------	----------------------------
----------------------------	----------------------------
----------------------------	----------------------------
----------------------------	----------------------------

Note: _____

_____

_____

Lucca Travel Planner

Date: _____

Destination: _____

Address: _____ Transportation: _____

What To Do	Location

Note: _____
_____
_____

Lucca Travel Planner

Date: _____

Destination: _____

Address: _____ Transportation: _____

What To Do	Location
- - - - - - - - - -	- - - - - - - - - -
- - - - - - - - - -	- - - - - - - - - -
- - - - - - - - - -	- - - - - - - - - -
- - - - - - - - - -	- - - - - - - - - -
- - - - - - - - - -	- - - - - - - - - -
- - - - - - - - - -	- - - - - - - - - -
- - - - - - - - - -	- - - - - - - - - -
- - - - - - - - - -	- - - - - - - - - -

Note: _____
_____
_____

192

Lucca Travel Planner

Date: _____

Destination: _____

Address: _____ Transportation: _____

What To Do	Location
....	....
....	....
....	....
....	....
....	....
....	....
....	....
....	....
....	....

Note: ....
....
....

Lucca Travel Planner 🪐

Date: _____

Destination: _____

Address: _____ Transportation: _____

What To Do	Location
----------------------------	----------------------------
----------------------------	----------------------------
----------------------------	----------------------------
----------------------------	----------------------------
----------------------------	----------------------------
----------------------------	----------------------------
----------------------------	----------------------------
----------------------------	----------------------------

Note: _____
_____
_____

Lucca Travel Planner

Date: _____

Destination: _____

Address: _____ Transportation: _____

What To Do	Location
----------------------------------	----------------------------------
----------------------------------	----------------------------------
----------------------------------	----------------------------------
----------------------------------	----------------------------------
----------------------------------	----------------------------------
----------------------------------	----------------------------------
----------------------------------	----------------------------------
----------------------------------	----------------------------------
----------------------------------	----------------------------------

Note: _____

_____

_____

Lucca Travel Planner

Date: _____

Destination: _____

Address: _____   Transportation: _____

What To Do	Location
------------------------------	------------------------
------------------------------	------------------------
------------------------------	------------------------
------------------------------	------------------------
------------------------------	------------------------
------------------------------	------------------------
------------------------------	------------------------
------------------------------	------------------------
------------------------------	------------------------
------------------------------	------------------------

Note: _____

_____

Printed in Great Britain
by Amazon

40512804R10109